DOUBLE TAKE

A Second Look
at the Joy of Seeing

- an artist's illustrated memoir -

BOBBIE HERRON

Double Take

Copyright © 2022 by Bobbie Herron

Written and illustrated by Bobbie Herron

Published by FreedomWeavers Studio Press

ISBN: 978-1-7358730-2-2 (paperback)

ISBN: 978-1-7358730-3-9 (eBook)

Library of Congress Control Number: 2022912905

All rights reserved. No part of this publication may be reproduced, distributed, or transmitted in any form or by any means, including photocopying, recording, or other electronic or mechanical methods, without the prior written permission of the publisher, except in the case of brief quotations embodied in critical reviews and certain other noncommercial uses permitted by copyright law. It is a copyright infringement punishable by law to reproduce any of these images without written permission from the publisher. Some names and characteristics have been changed, some events have been compressed, and some dialogue has been recreated. Any perceived slight of any individual or organization is purely unintentional.

For more information, visit FreedomWeavers Studio Press at our website: www.aloftwithinspiration.com

Dedication

I dedicate this book to Charlie Mackesy, whom I've never met.

On November 3, 2021, I was snuggled up on my couch, a cup of cocoa in hand, listening to Mr. Mackesy's recording of his enchanting bestseller, "*The Boy, the Mole, the Fox, and the Horse.*" I slowly turned the pages in my hardcover copy, following along as he read aloud, loving every minute.

Something shifted inside me, my relief palpable.

"*I can simply write the next book,*" the voice inside me said.

I could spend time and money taking one memoir writing course after another and, in doing so, turn this Book #2 into a chunk of granite dangling from my tired neck. Or, I can just sit down and have a chat with friends. A chat about this curious girl, me, who in

2020 wrote a book called *Look at That!* about looking at things—and sketching—then looking at things some more.

Three things are important to me, and may be helpful to you too:

1. I enjoy people who know that spreading kindness is the most important thing we can do.
2. I realize none of us do it perfectly. We bang into each other, get our feelings hurt, and sometimes hold on to resentments long past their sell-by dates. Yet there's hope, because,
3. We're all, every one of us, just one thought away from a fresh outlook. Perhaps even a double take.

Table Of Contents

Preface: A Return to Joy · 1
Introduction · 3

Chapter 1 - 2013: A Gentle Possibility · 9
Chapter 2 - 2014: Gaining Momentum · 19
Chapter 3 - 2015: Settling into a Rhythm · 51
Chapter 4 - 2016: A Show, Then Travel! · 67
Chapter 5 - 2017: Early Warning Signs · 91
Chapter 6 - 2018: A Sisyphus Year · 121
Chapter 7 - 2019: Endings and Beginnings · 153
Chapter 8 - 2020: A Booklet? Possibly a Book? · 185

Epilogue · 217

Merriam-Webster

double take

dou·ble take | \ ˈdə-bəl-ˌtāk \

A delayed reaction to a surprising or significant situation after an initial failure to notice anything unusual

usually used in the phrase, do a double take

Preface: A Return to Joy

In 1992, I quit drawing and sketching forever, or so I thought. Two decades later, on January 24th, 2013, I heard a radio interview with Danny Gregory that changed my life.

At the time, I didn't know who Danny Gregory was; I was driving my car, listening to a favorite talk show. During the interview, the NHPR host asked Danny about the role that sketching played in his life. Danny's answer was casual and eloquent.

He described how he'd worked for many years in advertising in New York, and carried an inexpensive sketchbook with him, a normal tool of the trade, that he used for taking notes while brainstorming with clients, colleagues, as well as jotting down random campaign ideas throughout the day. Like me, he could think better with a pen in his hand.

One day, a life-altering family tragedy occurred. His wife was badly injured, and suddenly Danny became the sole care-provider for their toddler son while his wife was being cared for in the hospital.

He told a story about one day, when his son had just gone down for a nap, and Danny suddenly felt overwhelmed. Without thinking, he picked up his sketchbook and a pen, sat down, and just stared at the items on the shelf in front of him. He began tracing the edges of the items, not really drawing them, just slowly doodling the shape of the "skyline" of the bottles. After a few minutes, he noticed two things: there was a very wonky sketch on the page in front of him, and for some mysterious reason, he felt a little less overwhelmed. I smiled. I knew that feeling.

The radio interview ended, and I finished my drive home. The next day, I walked to my local bookstore, Gibson's, and found a copy of Danny's book, *Everyday Matters*. The book felt like a secret talisman in my hands. I carried it to the checkout counter and thought, "Perhaps this is the key I need to unlock my heart, to return to sketching for joy, not results. Maybe I can learn to play again."

I had left drawing and painting and my identity as an artist behind me twenty years prior, in 1992, because I was going blind. Suddenly, that didn't feel like a good enough reason.

Introduction

My blindness story began in 1975 when I was twenty-two years old. The problem was only discovered because I talk a lot.

On June 3rd, 1975, I was at my optometrist's office for a routine check-up, hoping for an updated lens prescription. Reading aloud the letters on the eye chart, I made the off-handed comment, "Gee, that's funny, it's darker out of one eye than the other."

The optometrist checked the optic pressures, something rarely done for a healthy young person. He muttered something about how his new equipment must be calibrated wrong because one reading was ridiculously high. Just to be safe, he referred me to a local specialist for follow-up.

A few days later, an ophthalmologist confirmed there was a serious problem. That year, I had four surgeries in my left eye and experienced a choroidal hemorrhage which I wouldn't wish on my worst enemy. It felt like giving birth through my eye socket.

You carry on though because what's the alternative? At twenty-two, any career dreams I'd entertained were crushed by these sudden eye surgeries as well as the uncertain prognosis from top Boston ophthalmologists. I knew one thing for certain: I needed to work, but moreover, I desperately needed health insurance. I settled for office jobs, praying it would only be a temporary situation.

Ten years later, my right eye was also diagnosed with glaucoma, but luckily it responded well to medication. It had been a full decade without a serious eye crisis, and I began to think the worst was behind me. Creative instincts were stirring, well beyond those survival instincts that had clouded my inner vision.

I was itching to return to my original passion, visual art. I'd been an art major in college, dabbling in a wide variety of media, including sculpture, weaving, ceramics, and drawing. When I discovered watercolor, in 1986 at thirty-four years old, I knew instantly I was home.

In the next six years, I became proficient at watercolor. I sold several paintings, had a one-woman show, and at times felt I'd found a new career path. I was joyful, focused, finally in my element. I was soaring.

During those halcyon years, I was only vaguely aware that my left optic nerve was silently continuing to deteriorate, despite reasonable optic pressure. Each "surgical insult" (a medical term that seems poetically accurate) had created its own set of damaging side effects, despite surgeons' best efforts.

Then in 1992, the last bit of sight in my left eye vanished. Suddenly I could no longer do what I'd worked so hard to be able to do: create sellable, high-quality watercolor paintings. I was making rookie mistakes. I'd be near completion of a painting, adding just one more foreground detail, and it would backfire. The wispy grasses I intended to paint were an ugly smear instead. Bad aim. I knew how to do this watercolor brush-dance, and I'd been good at it! What the heck!

"I'm used to painting with one-and-a-half eyes," I told myself. "Just because the fuzzy eye is now gone altogether, have I suddenly forgotten how to paint at all?" I kept on trying until I couldn't stand it. In the process, I created piles of tissues, stained with a blend of mopped-up watercolor mud and desperate tears.

No depth perception is no joke. No more free-spirited calligraphic marks. I no longer had the luxury of casual glancing or graceful mark-making; I had to study what I was looking at to calculate the distance from brush tip to paper. It was exhausting.

My despair was so great I gave up. At the time, I had so many other losses going on: the end of a marriage, the end of a job, the end of a way of life I had loved. I had no resilience left. I had to figure out what to do with the rest of my life. I faced starting all over, half-blind, at forty.

Over the next twenty years, there were seven additional eye surgeries to my left eye, as well as two on my previously untouched right eye. More than enough reason to leave all artistic ambitions behind.

Luckily, "giving up" didn't work, even during those two creatively fallow decades from 1992 to 2012. Creative expression is an internal pressure that must find release somewhere for all of us, whether it's through gardening, cooking, woodworking, creating a home, or raising a family. There are many outlets, but stopping it is not an option; it's the life force itself. Even though sketching went by the wayside for a couple of decades, writing never did. A pen is my favorite archeology tool for discovering what's buried deep inside. At times, it feels like wisdom is coiled up inside the barrel of my pen, like a long string of licorice, just waiting to uncurl.

In 2013, sketching and painting came back into my life thanks to the catalyst of Danny Gregory's NHPR interview. Looking back over these past thirty years, I see that, through it all, I was creating raw material for this book.

I've thoroughly enjoyed rereading my forty-plus sketchbooks and journals as I've worked to compile this artist's illustrated memoir. I smiled as I witnessed this person, me apparently, stumble and grow and give up and push through, muttering her way to discovering a peace and confidence I never thought possible. At times, I barely recognized "her."

"No one gets out of this life unscathed," a dear friend reminds me. I hope that by reading this story, you will see more clearly your own inner resilience, which you have exercised over and over again, perhaps without fully honoring it. Your dent is your gift. Embrace it, and carry on, gladly.

Chapter 1: 2013

A Gentle Possibility

January 23, 2013 - Wednesday evening

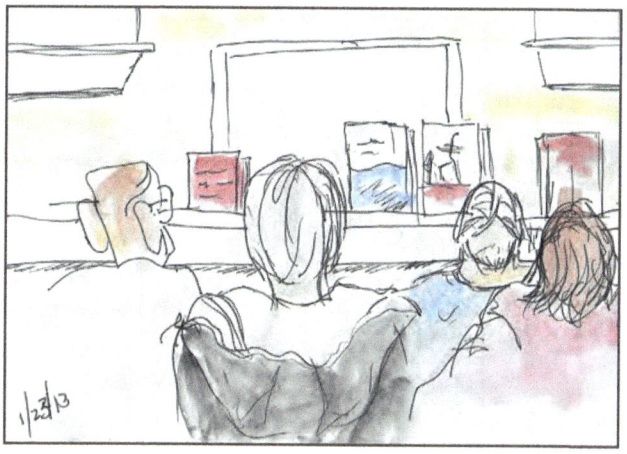

[Note: I did this simple sketch while sitting in a meeting, listening better because I had a pen in my hand. The very next day, I heard Danny Gregory's fresh answer to the question, "Why bother sketching?" I began carrying a sketchbook with me everywhere. It became my lucky charm, triggering an inner smile whenever my hand brushed across it in my shoulder bag. I put together a basic travel art kit too, small yet containing everything I needed. My brand-new sketching output increased exponentially.]

March 22, 2013 - notes while sitting in a meeting

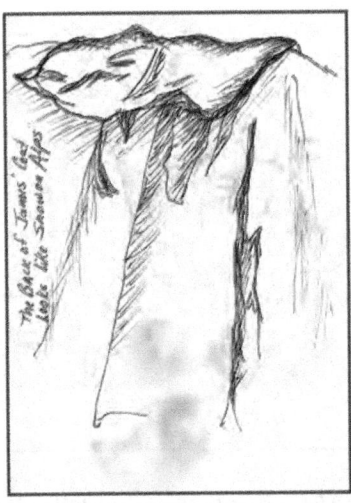

The back of James' coat looks like
snow on the Alps.

April 8, 2013 - Monday 2pm- Clinton Street Concord NH

Although unseen, there are school athletic fields just beyond this barn in Concord, so the soundtrack of this bucolic scene features the shrill cries of children exercising their young lungs. The boys growl and grunt, the girls holler at a far higher pitch, and another generation of energy is born.

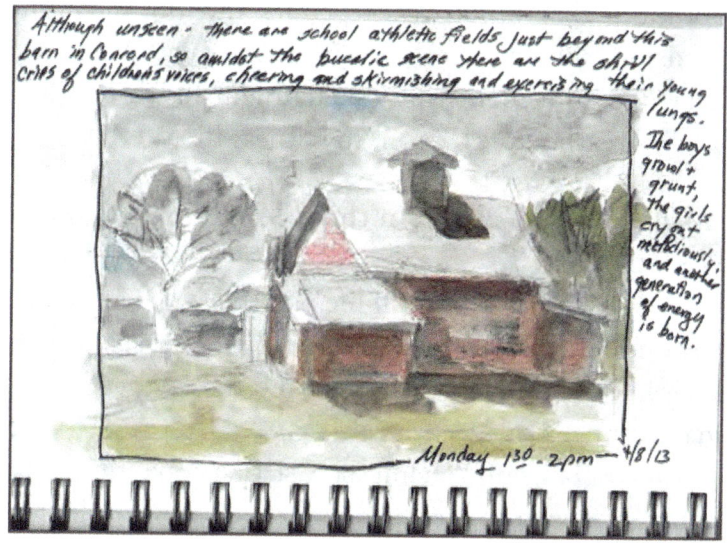

[Note: Not long after I created that sketch, those barns of that family farm were torn down to make room for more athletic fields. One day, I was out having coffee with a friend, and she happened to see that page in my sketchbook. She gasped. "I know the daughter of the farmer who owned that place. I've played in that hayloft! Could I buy a copy of your sketch to give her? It would mean so much to her and her family."

I made a print the next day, and gave it to my friend as a gift, of course. You never know when you'll make someone's day, just by pausing to draw something that caught your eye.]

April 16, 2013 - Lunch at the Barista in Bicentennial Square

Today is the day after the Boston Marathon

bombing that killed three people and injured hundreds. Normalcy is relative and temporary. When my heart is aching, sometimes sketching helps. It reminds me to breathe, to carry on, to witness life.

April 22, 2013 - Back in the café- sketching and writing

Years ago, I did two still-life paintings, one of onions and one of mushrooms. After finishing the two paintings, I felt like a murderer when I cut into those vegetables to make dinner!

I have that same feeling now. I first took a bite out of my sandwich to create an interesting view of the lettuce and cheese and tomato inside, so I could draw my beautiful lunch. It felt like an artist's version of saying grace, to sketch my meal before eating it. I finished the sketch, and the problem now is I feel I'm destroying something by simply eating my lunch! There's a spiritual lesson here somewhere.

April 27, 2013 - Another great lunch at True Brew Café

Here's a lesson most urban sketchers learned ages ago: If you're going to sketch your lunch, get a side order as well as the main dish, so you can eat and draw your lunch at the same time!

Another thing I've noticed: café dining offers a false sense of privacy to diners, and sketching is a brilliant cover for unadulterated eavesdropping. Two young professional women are sitting at the next table—one of them is very soft-spoken and attentive while the other is driving the conversation. The latter one is talking so steadily, so passionately, she certainly has tasted none of the food she's eaten. The focus is on money, conflict, black-and-white thinking, a lot of head but not a lot of heart. There's such a difference in volume between the two of them, the friend speaking quietly, confidentially, while the lawyer/attorney (I seem to have given her a profession!) is louder, more right, more insistent, more self-assured.

I cringe as I wonder how often I've been in a café with a friend, and unknowingly taken on either of these two roles. A sobering reminder to be aware of my surroundings, not just for physical safety, but to respect privacy as well.

July 9, 2013 - Beautiful day at I-89 rest stop

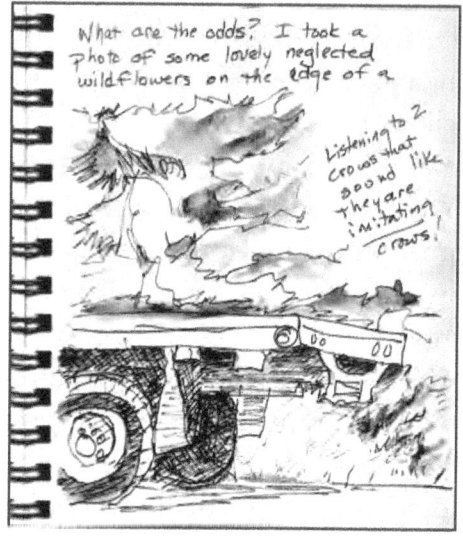

What are the odds? I took a photo of some lovely wildflowers on the edge of a rest area. I began to sketch them when a huge truck picked exactly that spot to pull up and park! I had to laugh. I'm also listening to two crows who sound like they're imitating crows!

December 31, 2013 - at The Museum of Fine Arts in Boston

Alone. This is my favorite way to experience a trip through any museum or gallery—alone with strangers, and not too many of those at a time, either.

I've been here about three hours, and I've only been in the John Singer Sargent watercolor exhibit area. That's the only reason I came here today. I just left the gift shop where I bought a book of postcards of his watercolors, and a not-so-great watercolor brush with "Sargent Exhibit/MFA" embossed on the brush handle. Touristy, not very useful, but I like it anyway.

When I arrived at the Museum this morning, after taking a long bus ride, the T, and a bit of a walk, an odd familiar feeling crept in. The closer I got to the exhibit hall, the more I felt tears prickling up through my nose and cheekbones. I had to stop at the head of the stairs to wipe away the tears of anticipation. I did the exact same thing twenty years ago, at the Georgia O'Keeffe exhibit in Washington, D.C.

When you feel a deep, heartfelt connection to people who lived mostly before you were even born, it's mind-boggling to be in the same room with something of theirs, something they actually touched, something that touched their hearts in return. I bet only practicing artists understand this, that a conversation happens between the artist and the canvas / paper. We don't tell the paper what to do; we talk back and forth, and we both listen! Our paintings become our old friends.

I feel so odd at times like this, like I'm missing a layer of skin that everyone else was given at birth. As my playwright friend Peter Stone used to say, "'Tis that gift of perception; it's both your glory and your burden." Embarrassing as heck some days.

Chapter 2: 2014

Gaining Momentum

[Note: Those mixed emotions and tears on New Year's Eve at the Museum of Fine Arts were the perfect prelude to 2014. I spent much of Spring 2014 sorting, discarding, donating, and packing all my worldly goods so I could move somewhere closer to downtown, closer to public transportation. As it turned out, I also joined a brand-new online school, created a one-woman art show, traveled across the pond and back again, celebrated an opulent wedding, and was stunned by a sudden death, all in one year. It's a good thing we never know what's just around the corner.]

March 30, 2014 - sketchbook thoughts

I have to laugh at how blissfully wonky my latest drawings sometimes are. In my sketchbook, I just follow wherever my eye leads; invariably, the drawing runs off the page. No consideration for design, balance, contrast, composition—all that art-school stuff—just spirit, just joy. I started a sketch today thinking I was drawing a church, but in the end, I only drew the top part of the steeple. And I love it; go figure!

This little sketchbook has served me so well. I started it in 2005, then put it down for seven years, filled two or three pages in 2012, and the rest has been completed since 2013 when Danny Gregory's book tapped me on the shoulder and said, *"Hey kid, wanna go outside and play?"*

Nothing's been the same since. I'm so grateful!

March 31, 2014 - sketching people

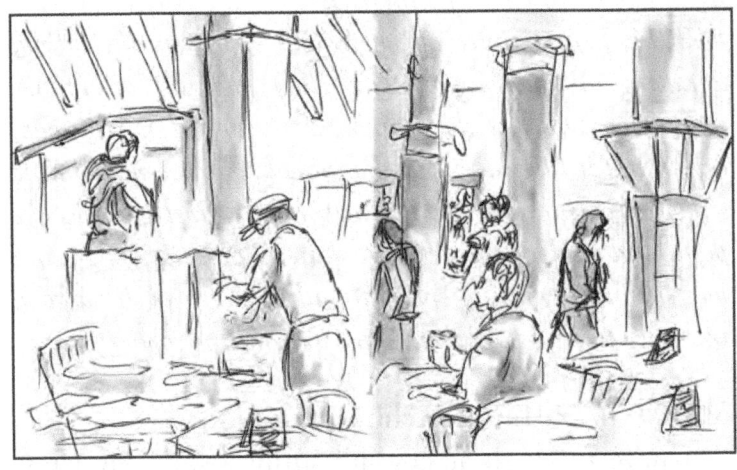

I came to the food court at the mall today to get over my insecurity about drawing people. Most of the "Food Court" was empty, many food stalls closed, hardly any shoppers. The good news is if you draw the same few people repeatedly from different angles on a two-page spread, you can create the illusion of a bustling economy!

April 4, 2014 - Sketchbook Skool begins!

I'm so excited to be a member of the maiden-voyage class of Sketchbook Skool, a brand-new alternative on-line art school started by Danny Gregory and Koosje Koene.

The first six teachers are fascinating, with quite varied styles. Each one believes that creative expression is for all of us, just like it was when we were little kids. Any hobby, or passion, has to be fun to be sustainable. Yes!

April 10, 2014 sketchbook entry

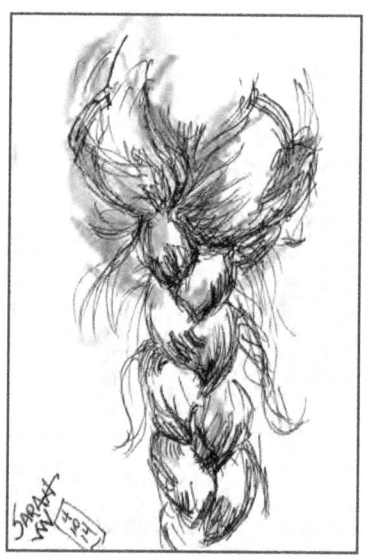

Sarah's Braid: At long meetings, always sit where the view is interesting.

April 14, 2014 - sketchbook humor

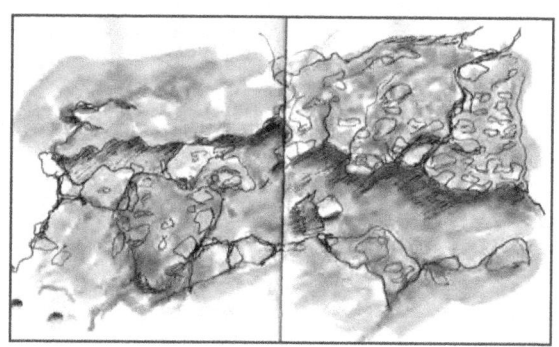

This felt like studying cartography—The Mediterranean Sea floor perhaps, or Saudi Arabia, or deep chasms in the Black Sea. In reality, it's just another New Hampshire pothole in April—complete with cigarette butt.

April 20, 2014 - sketch in tiny 3.5 by 5.5-inch Moleskine sketchbook

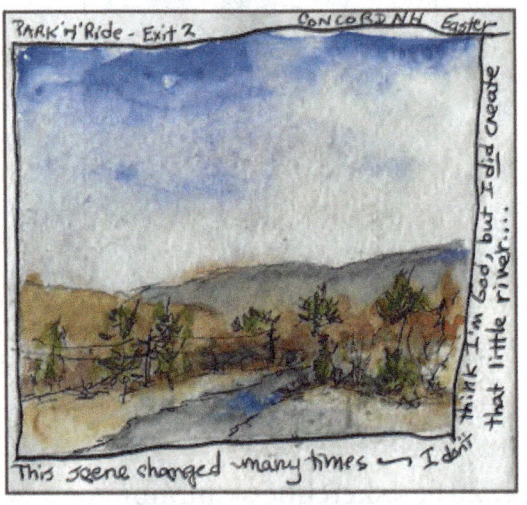

This scene changed many times; I don't think I'm God, but I did create that little river…

April 20, 2014 - Easter Sunday in East Concord
Unexpectedly beautiful day, possibly 70°F.

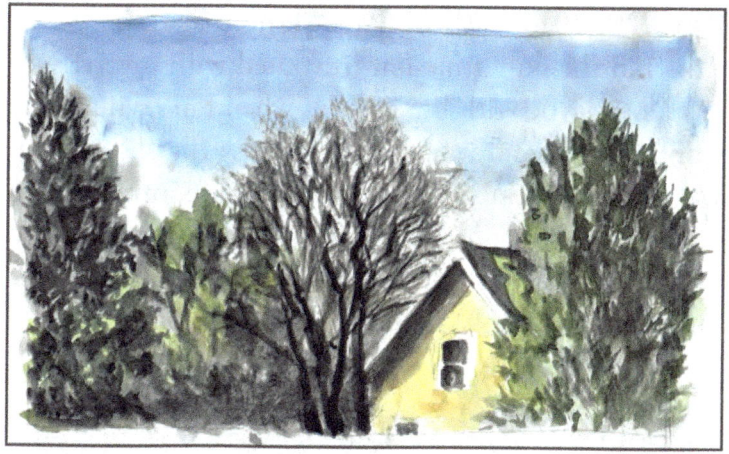

What I'm learning:

- The weight of the paper determines how cooperative the watercolor washes will be.
- Painting outdoors, even with the gentlest of breezes, means the paint dries fast everywhere: on the paper, on the mixing tray, and in the palette pans. Use a mist sprayer often!
- Not seeing or feeling the point-of-contact of the brush-tip makes it harder, but it needn't make it a miserable experience.
- I gave up on this sketch of the yellow house repeatedly, but those "giving up moments" disappear beneath the final enjoyable ones.
- Eyesight of any kind is a gift any day. Documenting sight by sketching is the frosting on the cake.

April 29, 2014 - White Park slanted sketch

I find the only time I'm frustrated with my art supplies, or maybe with life itself, is when I'm trying to do things the "right" way. When I throw that notion out the window, I realize that my imagination, my ability to invent my own rules, is the real superpower. I wanted to show the height as well as the breadth of this scene, but this sketchbook is small, and an awkward 3.5 by 11 inches when opened out.

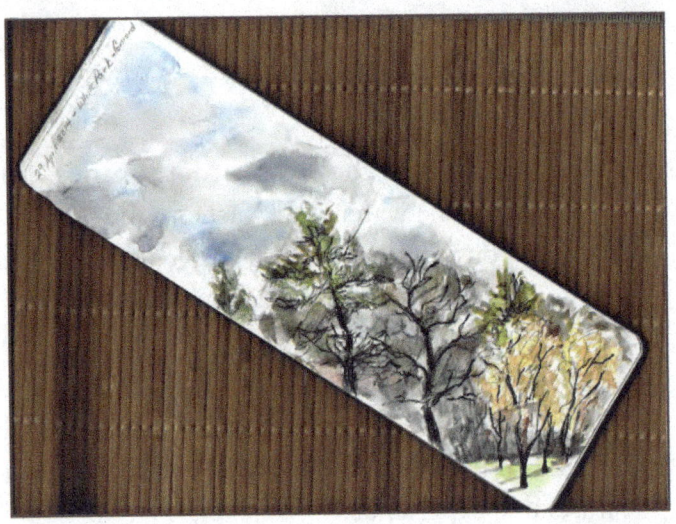

So why not say "No!" to both portrait and landscape formats? Et voilà, "port-scape", or perhaps "land-rait"!

May 1, 2014 - noon, three weeks after Sketchbook Skool began

Clearly, I have lost my mind. I've only been back in the land of sketching and painting for about a year, after a 20-year hiatus, and I just signed up to have a month-long, one-woman show of paintings in October, less than six months from now. Not one of those twenty-plus paintings even exists yet, nor do I own a single frame! I can lovingly blame Sketchbook Skool for this madness, especially Prashant Miranda's infectious underlying message of *"Why not? Enjoy!"*

I was thinking of Prashant while looking at the art display at my favorite café today, and suddenly that quiet voice inside me smiled and said, "Why not?" That voice isn't always very smart (I have proof of that!), but this time... yeah, why not!

May 7, 2014 - sketchbook observations

I'm amazed at what I learn when I look back through my old sketchbooks. I was flipping through one of them just now and came across a loose, playful sketch of a hillside, dirt road, and beautiful blue sky. Then I read the caption telling how dissatisfied I'd been at the time with the finished result. How sad!

Maybe this is the human condition regarding our own creative efforts: we have our initial intentions before we pick up the brush or pen; our idea of what the final image will look like. When our dexterity falls short of our excellent taste, or the wind picks up, or an unintentional brush-wiggle happens, we may think we're off course, when in truth, we may have just received an answer to the lifelong prayer: "God help me loosen up!"

This is the reason to keep most of my work in a good quality sketchbook rather than on random sheets of loose paper. Here, in my sketchbook, everything is automatically "good enough," chronological, private, and safe without being precious.

Another pattern I see, one that makes me chuckle, is a total lack of Watercolor Palette Fidelity: I refuse to marry just one! I keep trying to simplify my selection of colors, as well as the physical palette itself. I must own over a dozen different sizes and shapes of metal and plastic palettes. How embarrassing, how exciting! I can spend hours rearranging the half-pans and full pans into different palettes, all the while wondering if I'm the only one who does such a ridiculous thing. The only possible reason is that I want to paint, I have an urge to play with all those gorgeous colors, but I have no subject at all in mind... so I fiddle and rearrange and make color swatches, the same ones I've done a hundred times. It would be sad if it weren't so much fun.

May 20, 2014 - my second trip to much-loved England

2:35pm- I scheduled this ten-day trip several months ago, long before I signed up for Sketchbook Skool or that show in October. Why not do it all while I can, right?

This is the view from where I'm sitting in the Delta terminal of Logan Airport. I tinted the sky grey here and there before I decided to add color. Therefore, grey + blue = threatening weather, which is not the case! Two hours until take-off.

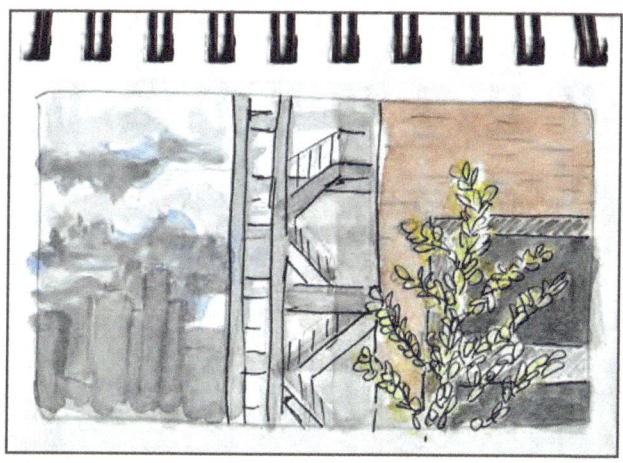

8:15pm- over the Atlantic Ocean, sketching and writing in the dark. The safety lights overhead resemble perfectly aligned stars; watching the flight map on the seatback in front of me is fascinating.

12:30am "body time," 6:30am local time, it's light out and I've been awake for 20 hours. The Super Airbus' landing here in Amsterdam was the gentlest I've ever felt. Amazing! Then the plane taxied more than 25 minutes, moving along at a good clip the whole time. I thought perhaps we were giving someone a lift to Brussels...

May 21, 2014 - Noonish, Wednesday

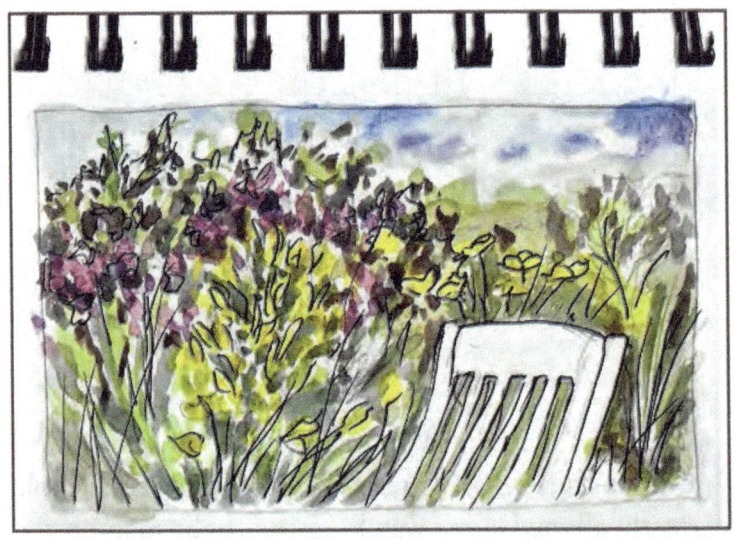

Lindeth Howe Hotel, Bowness-on-Windermere, UK. My suitcase has gone up to my room, but the room is not yet available, so I'm still self-contained in this little sketchbook. Nothing wrong with that. It's easy to forget how jet-lagged you are when you're enjoying gazing at a skilled gardener's work.

May 22, 2014 - Thursday, Troutbeck lunch

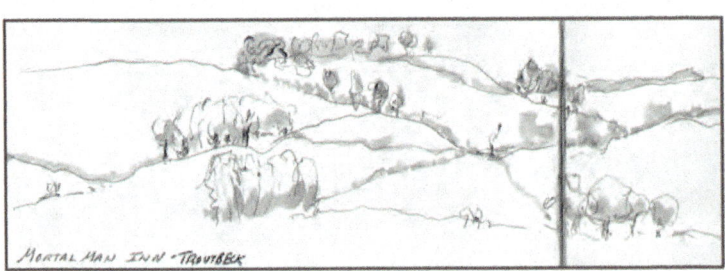

Only a few days into this trip, and my traveling companions are noticing it's normal for me to pull out my sketchbook when I have a few minutes to spare and a lovely view. Today is misty, rainy, overcast, and enchanting. The Mortal Man Restaurant is doing a wonderful job taking care of a coachload of hungry American tourists, and it's clear they are used to doing this. Tomato soup, fresh salads, and a choice of good sandwiches (cheese and pickle for me). The view out the window is every shade of green, and the interlacing of stone walls, hedges, and rolling hills mesmerizes me. I'm using my second sketchbook for this, a panorama format, somewhat intimidating 3.5 by 16 inches edge to edge when opened! So much to see and love.

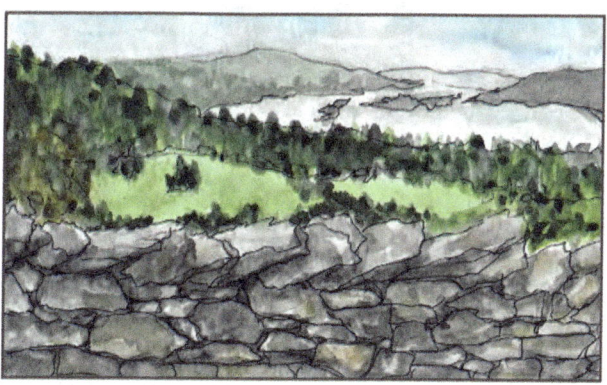

View from Troutbeck coach stop.

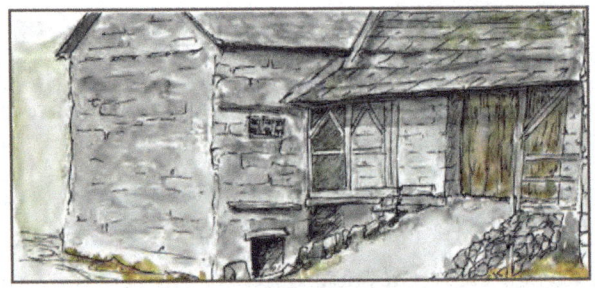

Townend barns- Troutbeck.

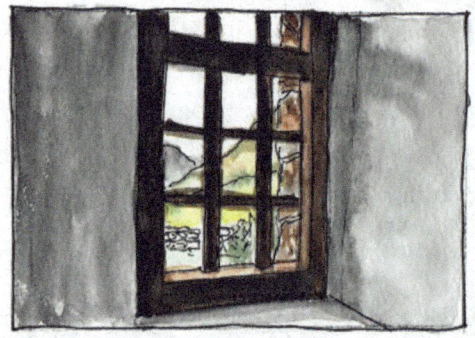

St. Martin's Church window, Cumbria, UK

May 23, 2014 - late evening

Yesterday was so busy, taking photos had to suffice. Poet William Wordsworth certainly had photogenic homes and gardens. It was a place near his home here at Rydal Mount that inspired his poem, "I Wandered Lonely as a Cloud."

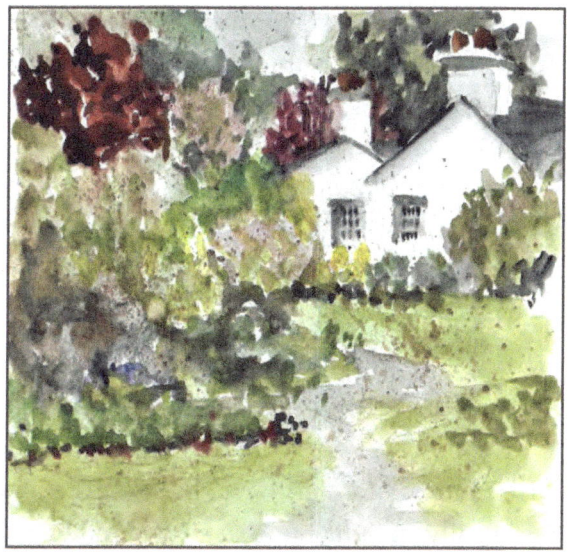

I did this sketch tonight using a photo I took yesterday.

May 25, 2014 - Sunday morning

Lately it feels like my small sketchbook jumps into my hands every time I have a spare minute. While our leader is desperately trying to herd up our straggling travel companions (a futile effort at times), I hear many members of my group fret that we will be "late," whatever "late" means when you're retired and on vacation!

I, on the other hand, am just standing here, close by the coach, noticing what catches my eye and doing a quick sketch. It actually adds a bit of excitement to not know how long I have to finish a drawing — it's "done" when the entire group is here and ready to get on the bus!

My only rule is to never, ever inconvenience the group, especially the tour guide and driver. Sometimes, after an initial introduction to the latest country manor or garden on the tour, we're given free time to explore on our own for twenty minutes or so. We're told what time to be back at the coaches, then all the group members scatter in different directions within the specified area, to scurry about and learn more. This is, by far, my favorite part of the Road Scholar experience. Armed with enough back story to have a good understanding of what I'm looking at, I scout about and find a place to sit where I'll be physically comfortable and mentally satisfied. Out comes my tiny travel art kit, often just a pen first, then I take the time to look around and simply breathe. I'm so lucky to have discovered this way of being more fully present, no matter where I am.

May 27, 2014 - Tuesday, farewell to Room 111

What a wonderful time Maggie and I have had in this stunning corner-view room at Lindeth Howe.

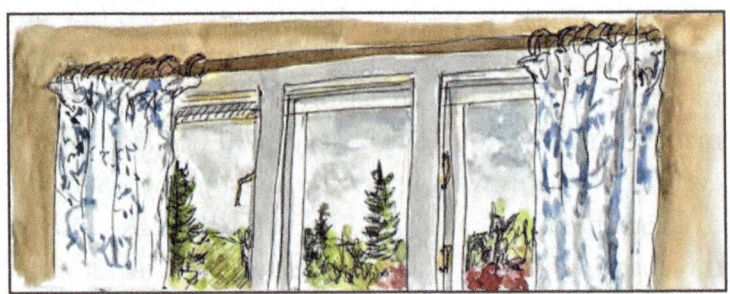

Tomorrow we are off through the Yorkshire Dales to Harrogate, a more urban destination, no less beautiful. Every day thus far has felt more like two or three days, with several beautiful and informative stops each day that have left all of us well satisfied. Our first six days here led us through sixteen estates, landmarks, and gardens, so yesterday's "free day" was a welcome rest for us all.

I took advantage of the free boat-ride up to Ambleside at the north end of Windermere and enjoyed exploring at a comfortable tempo with a fellow sketcher who was blessedly taciturn. I took lots of photos which will become paintings once I'm back home. That's my way of extending the trip, reliving moments via watercolor.

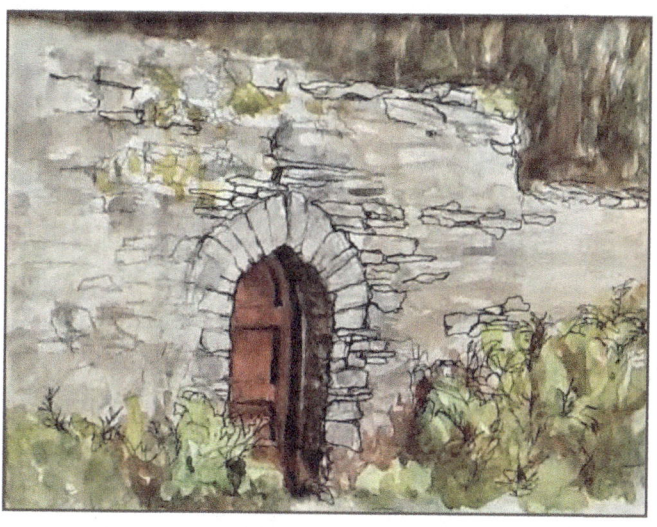

Garden wall and door, near Stagshaw, Ambleside.

May 29, 2014 - Thursday, 3:15 pm

We spent much of today riding around the English countryside, in an area unfamiliar to our driver/tour guide, Peter. He's an entertaining character, quick-witted and fun. We just came to a crossroads and paused a little longer than usual. One passenger said, "Peter, are we lost?" His reply: "I'd like to say it looks familiar, but once you've seen a stone barn and a tree..." We all laughed. There are worse things than getting momentarily lost in the Yorkshire Dales.

May 31, 2014 - afternoon

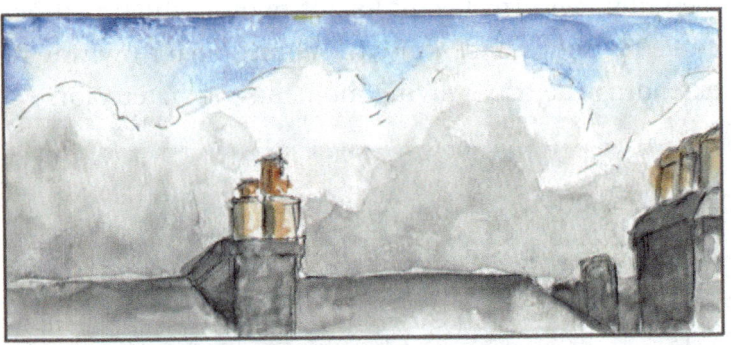

Proof the sun comes out in Harrogate... eventually.

June 3, 2014 - back home in New Hampshire, eager to travel more

This brief trip to England taught me so much. I gained a sense of personal confidence as an artist. I didn't need to come to England to paint, but apparently, I needed to come to England to have nothing else to do *but* paint. And since no one in England knew me, no one knew how much I was growing.

June 13, 2014 - on the bus to Boston

Heading into the city to visit the Isabella Stewart Gardner Museum at a leisurely pace. Traveling there by bus is usually a pleasurable, stress-free experience, but today the driver has a very unsteady ankle. The acceleration of the bus has a pulse all its own, regardless of the traffic in front of us; it'll be a relief to get to South Station! Then onward to the T, Red Line to Park Street, then the Green Line to the Museum of Fine Arts stop, then a bit of a walk. So many beautiful options for one day. The Gardner's courtyard is always appealing after a long, dreary New England winter. This ornate column, brick archway and frond-crowned tree were a pleasure to look at for the time it took to create this 3 by 5-inch sketch.

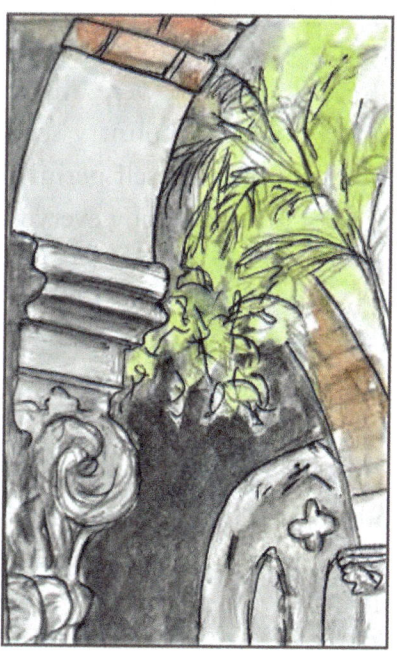

June 17, 2014 - notes in my sketchbook

I just realized I only pretend to crave art instruction. What I really crave is *art community*. Every adult art class I've taken has landed me in the middle of a delightful bunch of quirky, slightly shy, often-self-deprecating people who, like me, are just happy to be in a group of fellow sketchers, painters, and doodlers.

Today was no different—I joined a one-day workshop with Becky Darling, a talented local artist who is also a gifted teacher. I was the only newcomer; the rest of them had been with Becky for years, enjoying her instruction and the camaraderie that naturally forms in a group of older women who are all trying to befriend this beast called watercolor.

Most everyone was working on "quarter-sheets," about 11 by 15 inches. They were all using the same reference photo, an autumn country scene. Being just a visitor for the day, I gave myself permission to sketch something different and just enjoy everyone's company. I had brought with me my usual travel palette, a couple pens, a pencil, brushes, and a 9 by 12 block of stretched watercolor paper.

I decided instead to pull out my well-used, purse-sized Moleskine sketchbook (3.5 by 5.5 inches) and use that. The daylight streaming in the window was gorgeous, with a view out to a nearby granite-edged garden. The light and shadow on the windowsill called to me, so that became my subject.

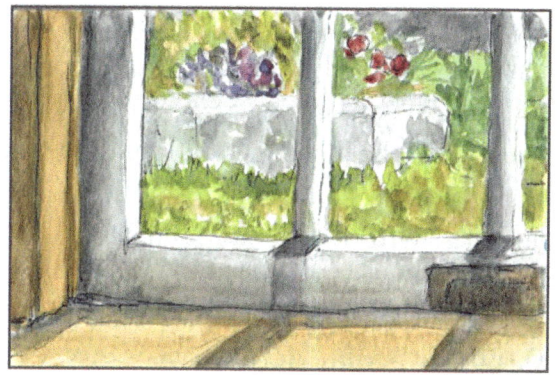

Toward the end of Becky's class, despite all the moaning and cries of "please, just another minute!" the time came for Show-and-Tell. Fond attentiveness filled the room as one-by-one we presented our work from the morning's session to the entire class, talked about how it went and where we had struggled. For many students, Becky had to kindly add at the end of their self-critique, "And the one thing you really like about your work today is…?"

One woman, Laura, had a strong New Hampshire accent which I thoroughly enjoyed. When it was her turn, she cleared her throat, took a deep breath, and exhaled a slow, "Ayuh…" She held up her work, which was quite good, and Becky proclaimed it a successful effort. Laura, uncomfortable with compliments, stood there as we smiled at her encouragingly. Finally, she cocked her head to one side, and declared, "Well, one thing I cahn say, it's good from afaah, and faah from good." Self-deprecation can be funny at times!

June 20, 2014 - gathering with friends

Some folks think if I'm sketching, I'm not listening to the conversation around me. Far from it. There must be a brain science explanation—all I know is that ladies who knit in meetings at church and elsewhere end up being the ones with photographic memories of everything discussed.

June 23, 2014 - people doodles

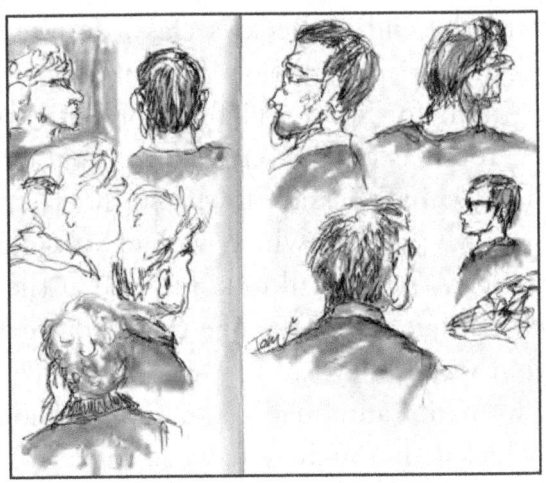

If you're shy about drawing people,
always sit in the back row.

June 24, 2014 - journal entry

Today was a landmark day. I saw my new home for the first time.

I've known for quite a while that I should move closer to town, to be closer to the bus lines, but apartments here are scarce and expensive. Today I met Jeff, the landlord, and we walked together up the two long flights of stairs so he could show me the apartment I'd seen on Craig's List. Jeff unlocked the door, walked in, and as I followed him, I gasped.

All I saw was light. The room had a ten-foot ceiling, two nine-foot-tall windows, cream-colored walls. A small but adequate open kitchenette was off to the left. That's it, a beautiful, big blank canvas, with tons of potential. Off to the right of the main room was a small bath, a small bedroom, and an adequate closet. But oh, that main room. Enchanting.

As I stood there, speechless, Jeff explained that the windows face north and that years ago, in the late 1800s, this entire third floor was unfinished, had been one enormous room. Back then, local artists had rented workspace up here, because the north light was ample and steady.

Jeff had no idea he was talking to an artist.

Before I left the apartment, I looked back over my shoulder and smiled. I heard a voice inside whisper, *"This is where she wrote that book…"*

"Who?" I asked myself. "What book?" It felt like I was touring a historic landmark, perhaps the home of a long-deceased famous author.

[Note: Six years later, I smiled when my first book was written, designed, and published from this very room, beside those very windows. Apparently the not-quite-famous author was me.]

June 28, 2014 - sketchbook notes

This afternoon we had the first meeting of the *Drawing Attention* sketchers' group here in Concord. I've been planning this since mid-April, hoping to offer beginning and experienced artists a way to meet and have fun sketching together, right here in our wonderful little city. The gathering is modeled after the international organization, Urban Sketchers. I named our little group before I realized that the Urban Sketchers' newsletter is also called *Drawing Attention.* Oh well!

Nine folks showed up for this first get-together. I've scheduled three more meet-ups after today, and I hope there'll be more.

As we started, I could see people's eager faces waiting to be told where we were going to be sitting, what to sketch, what supplies to use... oh my. "Urban Sketching" is such a mind-shift for people who are used to taking "art classes." Instead of offering a teacher's usual dive into minutia, my instructions were, "Go have fun!" I told them they were welcome to sit in the same area I was in, but that I was going to be sketching too, not teaching. We learn by doing, right? (That's the good news *and* the bad news!)

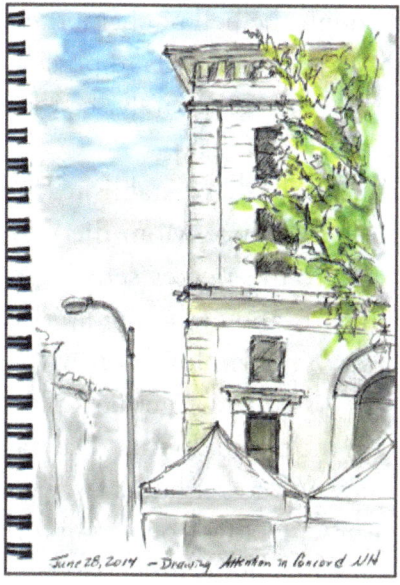

I like today's sketch of New Hampshire
Savings Bank on a farmer's-market Saturday.

July 28, 2014 - Monday, desperate news

I've been stopped dead in my tracks.

Here I was, racing along; it's two weeks until moving day, and there's a ton of work still to do. On top of that, my show at the café opens in about eight weeks, and I still have many paintings to complete. This afternoon the phone rang, and it was David [older brother], and after quick hellos, he told me to sit down and not interrupt him. He said he'd waited until after our niece's wedding two days ago, but now had to tell me that the cough, that he has had for quite a while, was not a symptom of his well-known early heart disease but was instead advanced lung cancer. At his wife's insistence, he was going to go through the hell of chemotherapy, to up his life expectancy from six months to possibly a few years. I can hardly write this, can barely see the page because I'm choking on waves of tears.

David and I have only reestablished a friendship in the last couple years, since Mom died, and now I feel like nothing in my life makes sense. How can I stay focused on painting, and gathering up fledgling artists, and doing all my self-employed creative work when I want to drop everything and get on a plane to see him? He's already told me not to do that, Dave and his infamous control issues. Whatever he wants, I'll do, but now a giant chunk of my already-crowded brain is filled with thoughts of him. I suppose if we weren't connected in some heart way, it wouldn't hurt so much, right?

Carry on, write, sketch, breathe. And conserve energy because next week I'm moving to my tiny third-floor loft apartment overlooking the city. A full forty-three steps up from ground level and no elevator. I can't think about that right now. Just carry on, and don't forget to breathe.

September 2, 2014 - sketchbook notes

There are so many pauses in a day, times when you're waiting for someone or something to happen: doctor's waiting rooms, waiting for the bus, dinner in a restaurant. Each one of these little nuggets of time can become a cellphone dive, or an aggravation, or possibly a window into a bit of time travel.

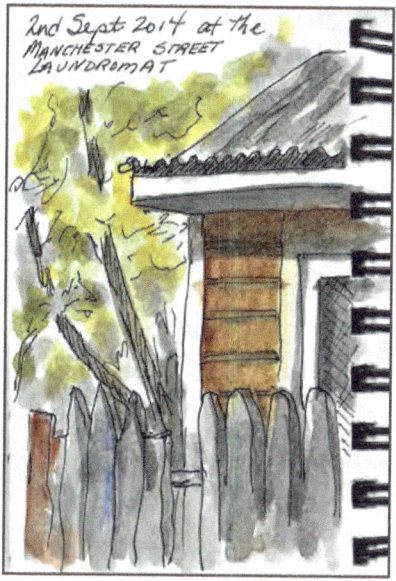

Sure, I could read a book while sitting at the laundromat or go run a dozen errands, trying to squeeze every minute for all it's worth.

Or I can stand outside, lean against a building, and sketch the laundromat building itself. I can even decide to change the color of the exterior from dull grey to a lovely golden glow.

My art show at The Works Café was initially scheduled for four weeks from now, but the manager just called to ask if I minded if he postponed it a month. Minded? I'm so relieved. No problem!

September 14, 2014 - Sunday

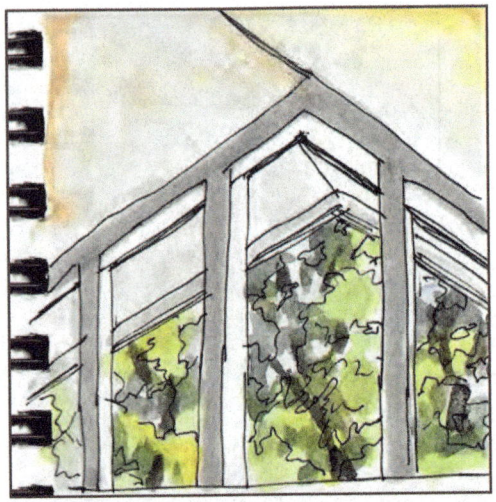

The peaceful changing seasons through this sanctuary window are a reliable delight.

October 23, 2014 - journal entry

    I'm chiseling away at all the work I need to complete for the upcoming show, and some friends have shyly asked, "No offense, Bobbie, but how can you create such good paintings if you can't see well?" It's almost like they're skeptical I have any trouble seeing at all.

    I get it. I smile and say that even my eye doctor doesn't see how I manage, and he knows exactly how gory my eye history is! I do it because, on a deep level, it feels like I can't stop, and I don't want to either. I work slowly because my one functional eye will water, glaze over, and lose focus repeatedly throughout the time I spend sketching.

    But in those little windows of time when I *can* see a

bit, it's exhilarating. The technical watercolor skills that I learned over 25 years ago are still with me. I've lost a lot of eyesight but thank God I've also lost that paralyzingly rotten habit of being overly self-critical.

Sketching is my thank-you note to the universe for the gift of any eyesight at all. No more, no less.

November 2, 2014 - Sunday morning, 5am

I'm up early; can't sleep, still buzzing over last night's turnout at my solo show downtown. I sold fourteen of the nineteen paintings within about an hour. Those attending were friends from church, my old weaving studio customers, old friends from far and near, and many total strangers. My niece drove all the way up from Boston, what an amazing woman she is. I've asked all the new painting owners to kindly leave their purchases on display for the entire month, clearly marked with "sold" tags, of course. Most galleries do that.

I feel like starting now to build up inventory for the next show. *"The next show"?* Wow, that wouldn't have even crossed my mind a month ago.

November 13, 2014 - eleven days later

I flew from Boston to here in St Paul, MN a couple days ago, on very short notice, to say my last goodbyes to my brother David. I've known for about three months that he was very ill, maybe dying, but now it's clear the chemo failed. They told him in August that without it, he would only make it to Christmas. Now, with the chemo, it looks like he'll die even sooner than that. He's so angry he wasted the last three months being "chemo-sick," instead of just struggling with lung cancer. Neither option would have been pleasant.

Dave and I have been estranged for so long, most of our adult lives, and if our brother Jon hadn't told me, I never would have known that David actually wanted to see me before he dies. Now that I'm here, I'm so glad I came. Dave goes in and out of being lucid. The early evenings are the worst because the late day shadows on the walls keep changing, and he becomes frightened. His brain no longer knows how to interpret the shapes, to tell the difference between solid and shadow. His family couldn't understand what he was seeing that upset him so, something that they couldn't see. I thought I'd give it a try.

I leaned over, put my face very close beside his, and said, "Dave, point to it." He did, and then I said, "Okay Dave, now trace it with your finger." As he moved his shaking arm, I could see what he saw, because my own eyesight is so abstract now, thanks to my lifelong visual struggle. Who would have thought lousy vision would ever come in handy?

I told Dave, "Yes, I see exactly what you see!"

He turned to me, shocked, relieved, and then he relaxed for the first time in over an hour. I gently explained to him that what was causing the optical illusion was nothing but late afternoon shifting shadows, and that I could imagine how scary it might appear.

He listened attentively, then quietly said, "Whatever you say, kid. It must be a Herron thing…" and drifted off to sleep in his hospital bed in the living room.

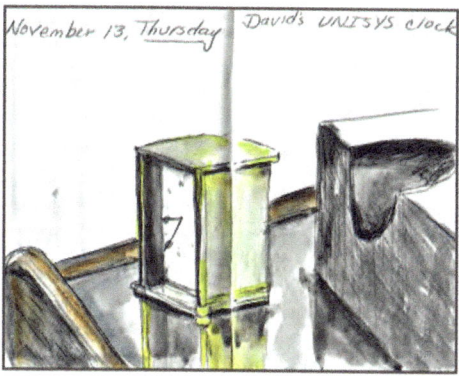

That's when I did this sketch of the little clock that was given to him as a tenure gift from his employer, and the ever-present box of tissues. Sometimes when emotions are running high, drawing helps. Self-soothing by sketching.

November 26, 2014 - thirteen days later

David Herron died this morning about 4:00am. That sentence is true, but it feels like science fiction. I'm still numb.

The holiday season feels so tainted with the deaths of my brother and my mom. Five years ago, Mom became ill in October and died three months later, on January 11th. David was sick for only a few months too and died Thanksgiving Eve. Their departures have left me disoriented.

Life has shoved me to the end of the family diving board. Chronologically, I'm next.

Chapter 3: 2015

Settling into a Rhythm

January 10, 2015 - notes in a new sketchbook

Sketchbook Skool classes online have changed my world in the last year; how amazing to have finally found my tribe, my community of people who appreciate looking at the physical world around them, no matter how humble the view. We sketchers take time to see what most people overlook.

Thanks to the Skool's global map, I've met two wonderful women right here in New Hampshire who are also Sketchbook Skool charter members. I've added a small pair of binoculars to my travel art kit, partly because of my eyesight, but also because the longer I look at anything, the more curious I become. Thanks to Dana, I've also learned to carry a felt-tip calligraphy pen, to loosen up my drawing, make it more bold, less fiddly.

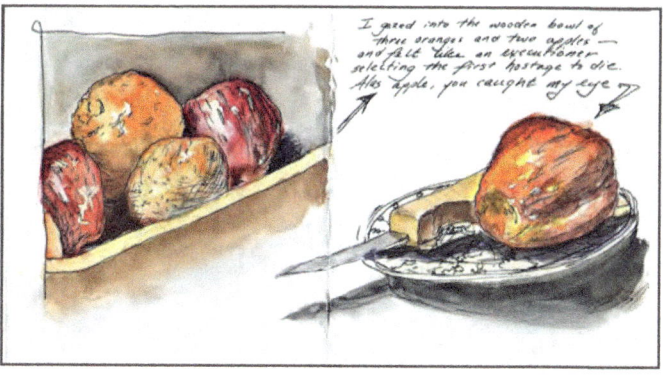

I gazed into the wooden bowl of three oranges and two apples--- and felt like an executioner selecting the first hostage to die. Alas, apple, you caught my eye.

January 13, 2015

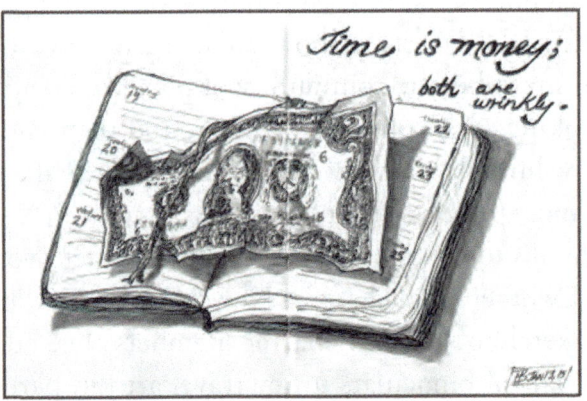

Time is money... both are wrinkly.

January 18, 2015 - sketching while listening at church

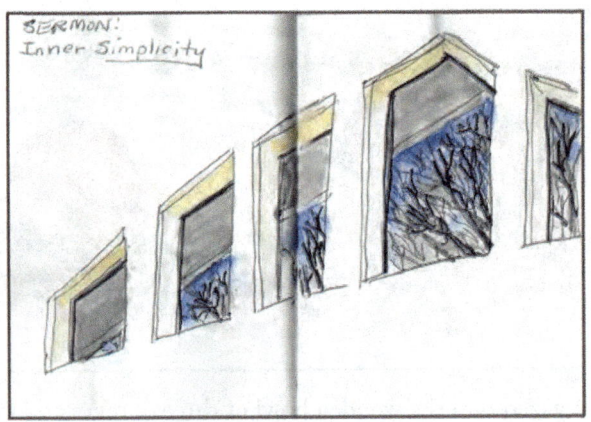

Calvin's beautiful piano music sounds
even better when I'm sketching.

January 19, 2015

Today I worked on a sketch of a gorgeous scene from a coffee-table book called *Walt Disney Animation Studios- The Archive Series: Layout and Background.*

My oldest memory of visual excitement was when looking at Disney animation backgrounds. Not the charming characters, not the animation itself, but the stills: the magnificent details in the background landscapes, interiors, close-ups of pots and pans, teacups, and candlesticks. I see the magic first, the techniques second. I bet this is where I fell in love with watercolor, without even knowing it.

January 29, 2015 - Thursday, late day magic winter light

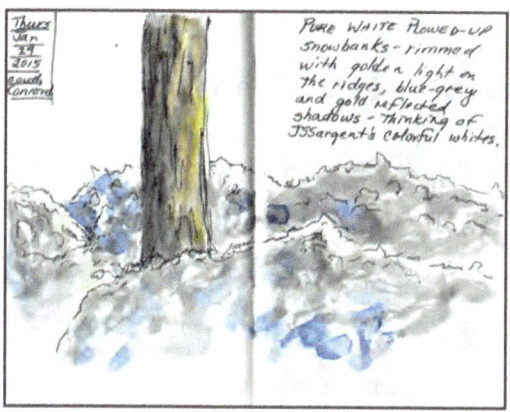

Pure white plowed-up snowbanks — rimmed with golden light on the ridges, blue-grey and gold reflected shadows — thinking of John Singer Sargent's colorful whites.

February 9, 2015

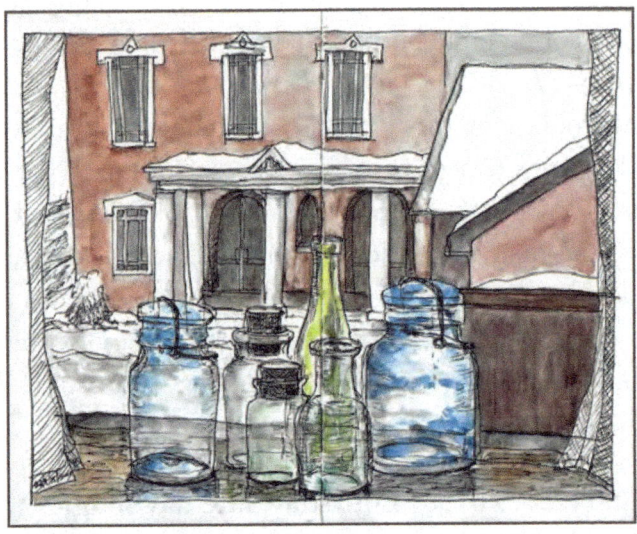

If you must face New England winters, be sure to have colored glass on your windowsills.

April 25, 2015 - journal entry about pens, and my own history

Back before gel pens, roller-ball pens, and even ball-point pens, there were only dip pens, then later, these wonderful things called fountain pens. Before World War II, pens weren't throwaway items, they were re-usable tools.

Refilling a fountain pen from a bottle of your favorite ink is a ritual: you simply can't rush through it without risking disaster. I still have my classic 1960s avocado-green Sheafer Skrip cartridge fountain pen; the dated color gives away its vintage. I bought it when I was in high school, and it still feels good in my hand.

Earlier today, I did something I thought would be impossible: I resurrected my dad's Parker fountain pen. The rubber-bladder filler system should have been beyond repair, full of dried out ink from 1967, the year he died. But thanks to lots of water and patience, it found new life this year, almost five decades later. I like the thickness of the line it makes. The balance and weight of the pen in my hand are oddly familiar and calming, like a DNA telegram from his hand to mine.

I think of Daddy holding this same pen in 1963, when he sat at his desk at home writing me those birthday checks for a party dress, or a trip to see Ice Capades in New York City. I still have those checks tucked away with my other ancient treasures. It's obvious he used this very pen to write them.

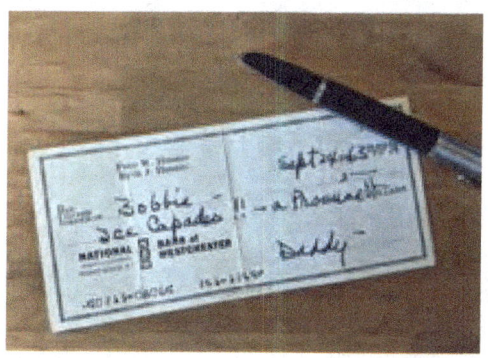

I feel a little ridiculous writing this, but I was in full pre-teen hero-worship mode when Dad died unexpectedly. It's such a gift to reconnect with him now, through his fountain pen that I thought had also died but has now found a new life and renewed purpose.

May 2, 2015 - sketchbook notes

I knew it was fun for writing, but wow, what this pen does for my sketching is amazing. The line is so expressive, and I can vary the line weight easily by having a lighter touch. With fountain pens, you barely press down anyway. With a featherweight touch, the line work becomes enchanting.

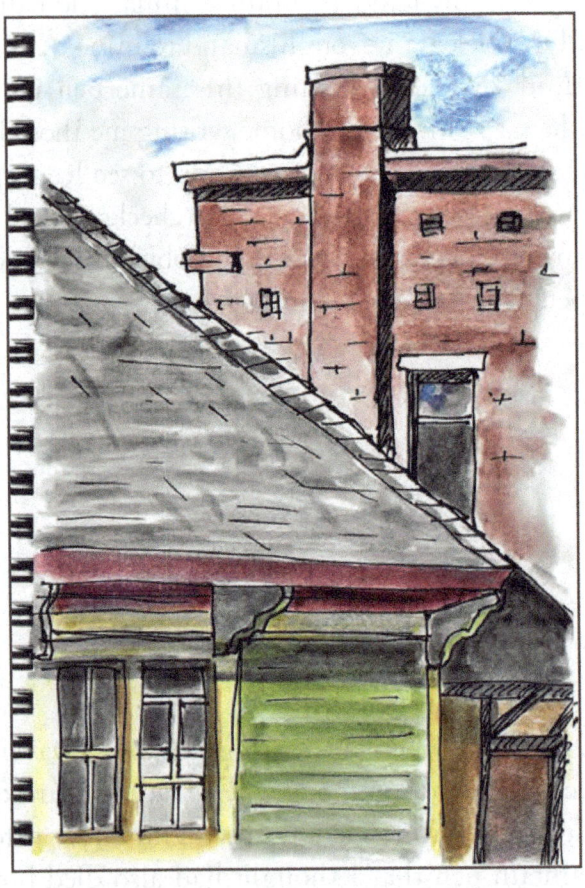

I wonder what Dad would think, seeing me sketching and writing with the same fountain pen he used at the Reader's Digest so many years ago. I like to think we'd be friends now, laughing together about how we each were so driven back then, while still so insecure, so in need of unconditional "hurrah" in our lives. We could shower each other with kudos now — and maybe through this pen, we are.

Later at Bicentennial Square

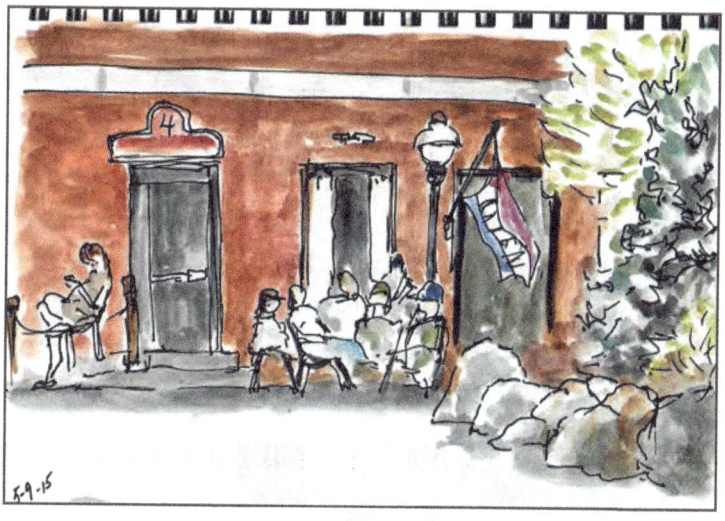

It's the perfect temperature outside for drawing today. All sorts of people have stopped to chat, nice for a change!

May 20, 2015

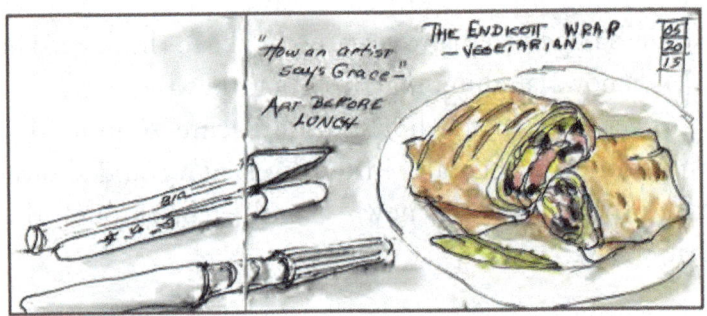

How an artist "says grace"—art before lunch.

June 17, 2015 - corner of State and School Street

Wednesday afternoon, on a perfect-weather day. I've been missing England, and I just discovered I can have a little taste of it by walking just two blocks from my home. The main church building was completed in 1904, and this annex was added much later, with a consistent style. It's funny, I just noticed the sketch looks like, "If Walt Disney went to England…" Definitely has a cartoon atmosphere!

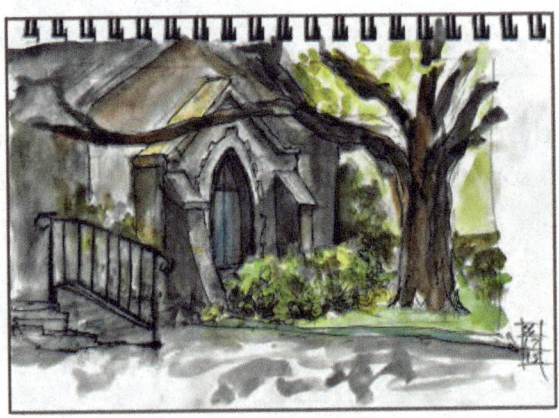

Here's what I learned:

- For something this complicated, it's easiest to use loose pencil first, then watercolor, then ink last.
- This sketch had several "adolescent" phases — times when I could have easily thrown up my hands in despair and "kicked the kid out." If I still had my old Inner Critic instead of my new Inner Shrug, there would have been a paper homicide.
- When it's breezy enough to be comfy outdoors, the paint dries quickly everywhere: on the paper, in the mixing areas, in the pans. "Water"color becomes "Dehydrated"color! That spray mister is useful throughout the process, not just at the beginning.

August 30, 2015 - sketchbook notes

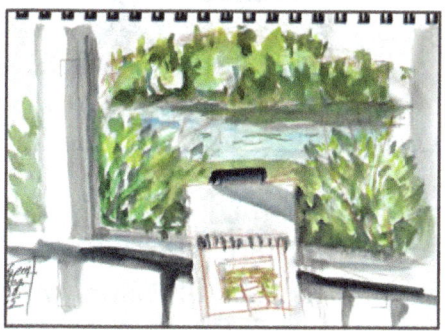

View from the cottage porch

I've rented a cottage for the week on my favorite lake in the world, Newfound Lake in Bristol, NH. I'm using it as an artist's retreat, to finally work through the course with Liz Steel that I paid for ages ago. The lessons are fascinating, and the view here is even better. There's no Wi-Fi near these cottages, so I'm working from a printout, and driving six miles into town each day to get my daily latte and to check email. This is a dream come true, paid for by all those watercolor painting sales, thank goodness.

August 30, 2015 - sketchbook notes

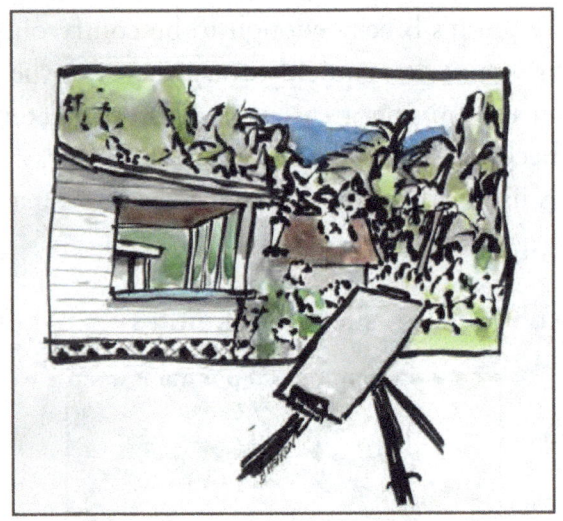

I just stepped outside to do a quick sketch of the cottage itself, line only, painting the color bits later. I discovered that I'm utterly out of control with the Pentel brush pen — no sense of when the tip will hit the paper, nor how huge a mark it will make when it does. The same is true with any brush for me, but the full-strength black ink here fairly shouts! I like the outcome of this sketch, but I held my breath through most of it. Ah, monocular life…

August 30, 2015 - evening light silhouettes

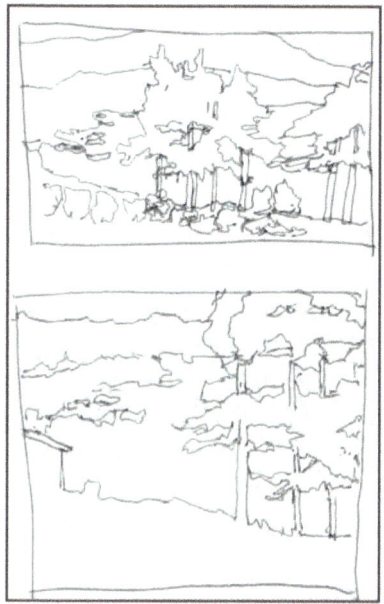

It's so much easier to see negative shapes right after sunset

August 31, 2015 - the next day

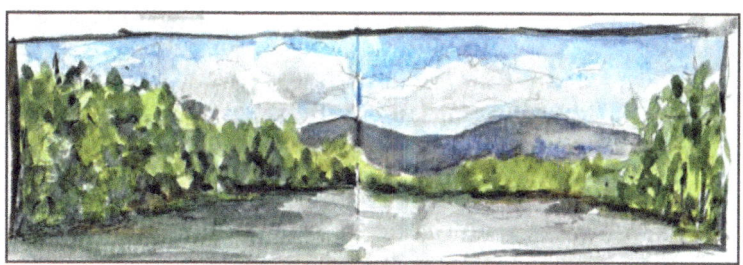

Newfound Lake always feels like home.

October 8, 2015 - note at the end of a discouraging sketchbook

I made it almost all the way through this sketchbook, a lovely red hardcover one with ivory paper. I bought it last year and have picked it up multiple times, tried to use it, put it down, and now I give up.

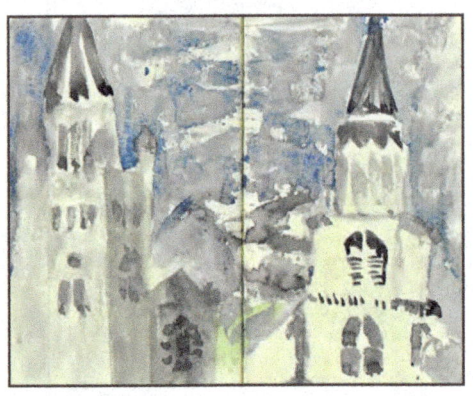

The paper is functionally water-repellent, which may be fine for colored pencil or pen sketching, but not great for watercolor! I think it may be clay-coated stock. The paint beads up on the paper, leaving an effect that looks like I used saran wrap or wax resist. Interesting effect, but not everywhere! And of course, whatever paint sits in bubbles on the paper surface takes forever to dry. So, I'm quitting now, twelve whole pages before the end of the sketchbook, with the declaration, *"Never, ever, waste time on unpleasant art supplies!"*

December 30, 2015 - journal entry

I've started using my timer more often, thanks to friends like Michael Nobbs. Timers can actually create a feeling of freedom rather than constriction, pleasant parentheses hugging creative time. It frees me from clock-watching.

    I start with the notion, "I want to deep dive into writing (or sketching) for 40 minutes, and then I need to get on with my day." Next, I wind up the mechanical timer on my desk, and I'm free to enjoy the work session. I love my old-fashioned wind-up timer that ticks along; it sounds like the pulse of creativity. The bell at the end is a single note of applause. "Yes, you did it!"

Chapter 4: 2016

A Show, Then Travel!

January 16, 2016

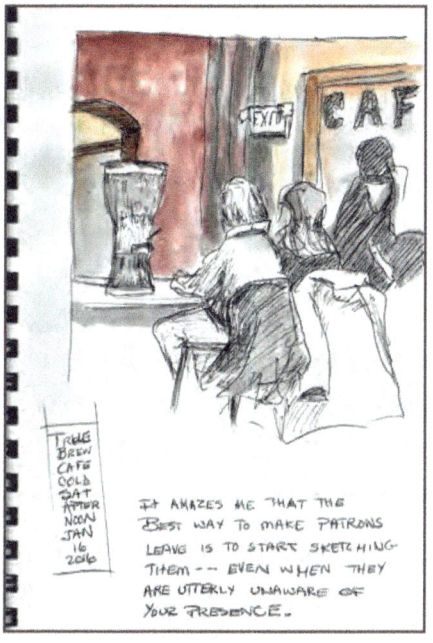

It amazes me that the best way to make cafe patrons leave is to start sketching them—even when they are utterly unaware of your presence.

February 27, 2016 - sketchbook notes

I sketched these curtains during a meeting tonight. I've almost lost my habit of sketching just for fun because I've been working every spare moment on pieces for the upcoming show in just a month, opening on April first. I'm excited that this style of ink drawing topped with rich watercolor is getting stronger all the time. The approach may look similar to the 2014 show, but wow, the experience of creating the pieces is vastly different. It's still hard work, but a lot less panicking, far fewer moments of, "Now it's ruined, what the heck!"

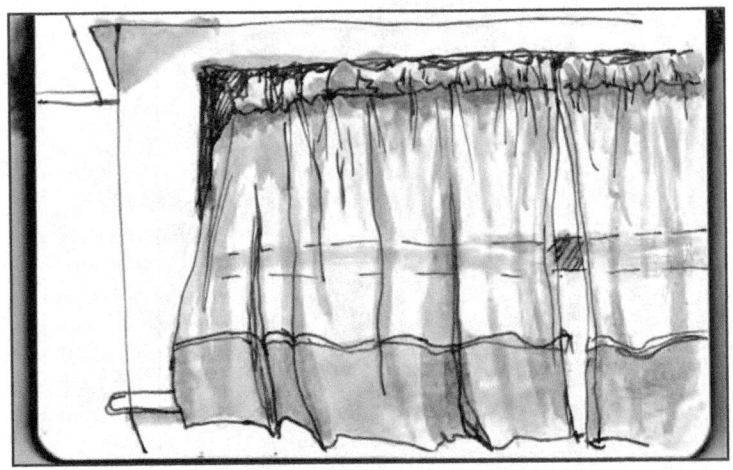

It's good to be back staring at tiny window curtains in church basements, just for fun. Puts a whole new slant on the expression "draw the curtains"!

March 19, 2016 - notes on the upcoming show

So far, so good. One sketch at a time, one splash of color at a time. Then signed, taped to a mat, the glass cleaned to a sparkle on both sides, framed, secured, tagged, and logged into a good old Excel document to be sure I'm on track. Two weeks to go.

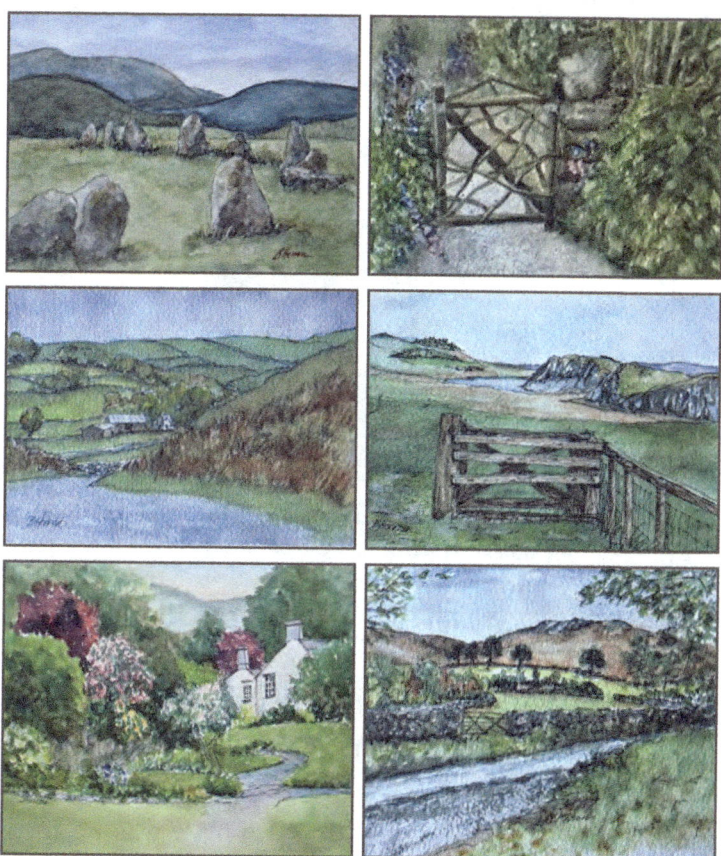

The entire show will be paintings of scenes from my two trips to England, beginning in the Lake District, then traveling north and east. I love the English topography, the atmosphere, the raw beauty of the North. Creating thumbnail photos like these and having them pasted here in my journal as well as on the spreadsheet, helps me stay organized.

April 1, 2016 – postcard announcement of the opening of my second show

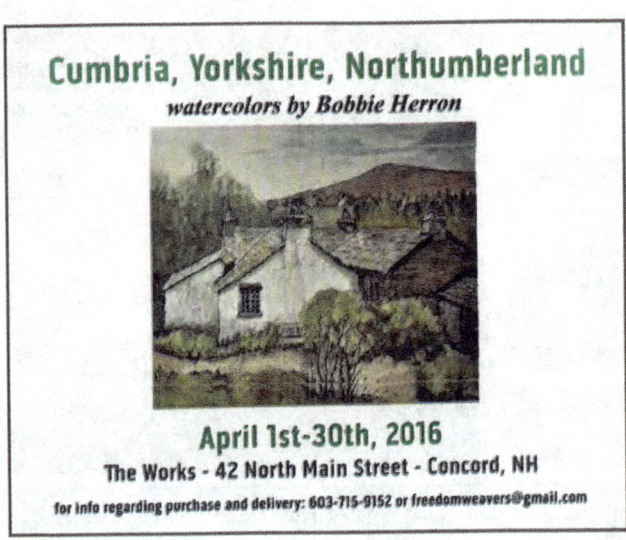

May 1, 2016 - journal entry

The month-long show is now over and I'm so pleased. I originally had fourteen paintings on display; eleven sold quickly, mostly on opening night. I was hesitant to let go of the painting of Wordsworth's Dove Cottage that I used on the publicity postcard, so just before the opening, I labeled it "Not for Sale." Such a relief! Some paintings are just too close to the heart for reasons I don't understand. Now for a well-earned exhale, then in three weeks, I'm off on my third trip to England, this time a garden tour.

I smile to think I thought that first trip to England in 2012 (a 60th birthday present to myself) was a "one-time-only" indulgence. Within hours of arriving, I knew I'd return.

England, especially in the north, felt oddly familiar, like a home I hadn't seen in a very long time. I pondered the possibility of genetic memory because Dad's mum was from Manchester, England. My first trip in 2012 explored the Lake District and Northumberland. In 2014 the focus was again the Lake District then on to Yorkshire. Now, in just a few weeks, I'm off to London, Kent, and Gloucester.

Many of the garden estates included in this upcoming tour would have fallen into disrepair over time were it not for the care and resources of The National Trust, which has been preserving places of natural beauty and historic interest since 1895. I'm lucky to visit England even once, let alone for the third time.

May 24, 2016 – about to leave for Logan Airport in Boston

I started this 80-page sketchbook journal in mid-March, in anticipation of this trip to England that officially begins today. I've jotted down my research notes right here in the sketchbook, creating two-page spreads for every stop, leaving the left-hand page blank. What a great way to make a 12-day trip last for three full months!

May 26, 2016 - sketchbook ponder after Day One of the English gardens tour

Still fully jet-lagged, but we're off to the Chelsea Garden Show—how insane! It is stunning sensory overload in every way. Over 150,000 people attend this massive garden show each year during five days in May. So well-organized, it's been in Chelsea since 1912, previously in Kensington, starting back in 1862. I'm glad I took loads of photos; they'll be great reference material for future sketches.

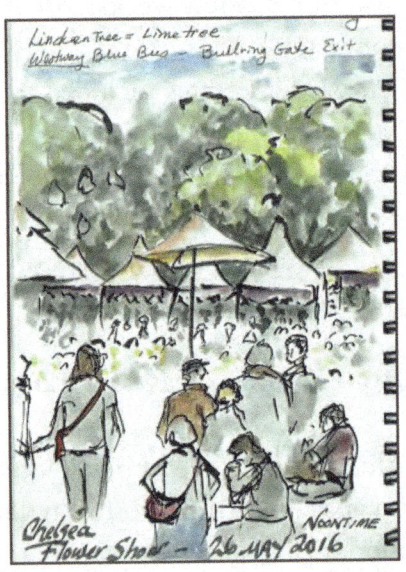

Later, in the shady area by the bandstand... I'm sitting in a lovely resting area, eavesdropping on four women picnicking in front of me. They sound and look like regular attendees, and sure know how to pack a wicker basket feast! The air is perfect here in the shade, the women's voices lilting, hovering, diving across two octaves of enthusiasm. I love being entertained while I draw.

May 29, 2016 - three days later, building momentum

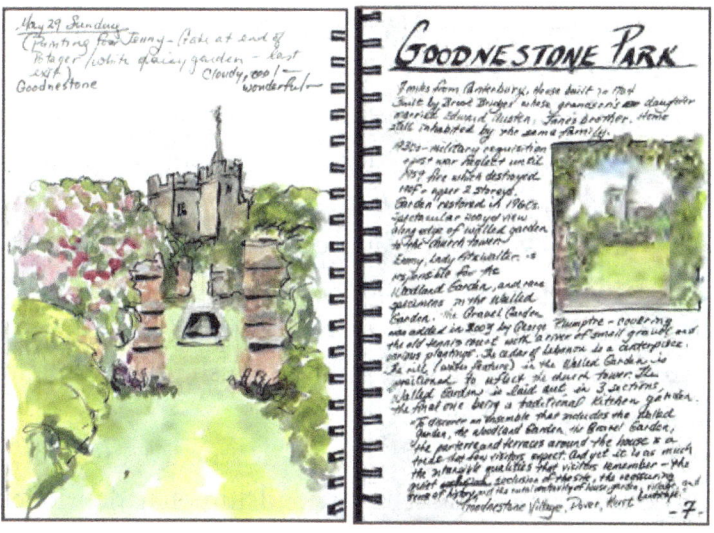

Despite being spelled "Goodnestone," it's pronounced "Gun-stun," of course, right? I created these detailed right-hand pages for each site while I was still back in New Hampshire. Day by day, I'm now filling the left-hand pages here in England, as we arrive at each location. The online research I did ahead of time has enriched the experience enormously!

May 31, 2016 - Day 6 of 11, English Gardens tour

This trip is so educational! Each morning our instructor gives us graduate-school-level lessons on the history of ornamental horticulture and landscape design across Europe and England, starting in the 1400s! It's fascinating and we're so lucky because she's retiring after this tour, retiring from both her work here at Road Scholar and her work lecturing at university.

The format of this tour is brilliant; we meet up in a conference room here at the hotel for the formal lecture in the morning to learn the day's lesson about the history of landscape design movements, and about sites that are examples of that era's tradition. Then, after a quick lunch, we all board the coaches and go to a site we have just studied. It's so exciting, every step of the way. All of us elders are taking scads of notes throughout class, as if we're preparing for an important final exam. The instructor has laughed, saying she wishes her graduate students were so keen.

In this morning's lecture, I learned a great deal more about the wonderful friendship that developed between Gertrude Jekyll, an experienced artist and plants woman, and Sir Edwin Lutyens (pronounced "Lutchins"), a young architect. Despite their 26-year age difference (they met when she was 46 and he was 20), they joined forces to become the first garden designer / architect team to collaborate rather than compete. They celebrated and benefited from each other's expertise, and the results were sublime in the one hundred plus gardens they designed together.

Today we visited RHS Wisley, a gorgeous place, but my rain gear was no match for the constant heavy downpours. I returned to the coach early, shedding my soaked-through raincoat and sweater. My umbrella was decorative at best against English downpours, oh well.

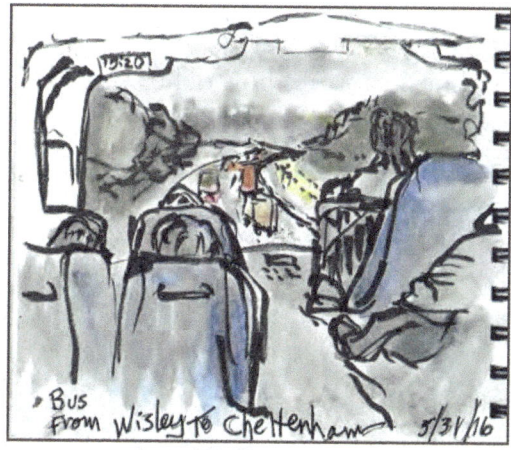

At least it was fun sketching in the coach on our way to the next stop, Cheltenham.

June 1, 2016 - Day 7 of 11, another gorgeous English garden

Yes! Finally, a stop on the tour where we listened to a brief welcome, enjoyed an abbreviated tour, then were left to ourselves to wander around the many gardens at our leisure for about thirty minutes. Perfect for me! I skipped some areas, of course, but I saw enough to know where I wanted to stop, stare, sketch, then paint.

While I was perching here in the beautiful Kiftsgate Court Gardens, I was also being observed by my traveling companion, Blake Caldwell. She took this photo of me while she was standing at a lower level. I had no idea she was there until she showed me this picture. I'm so pleased; it almost captures how deliciously snuggled-in I was feeling in my straw hat and blue raincoat.

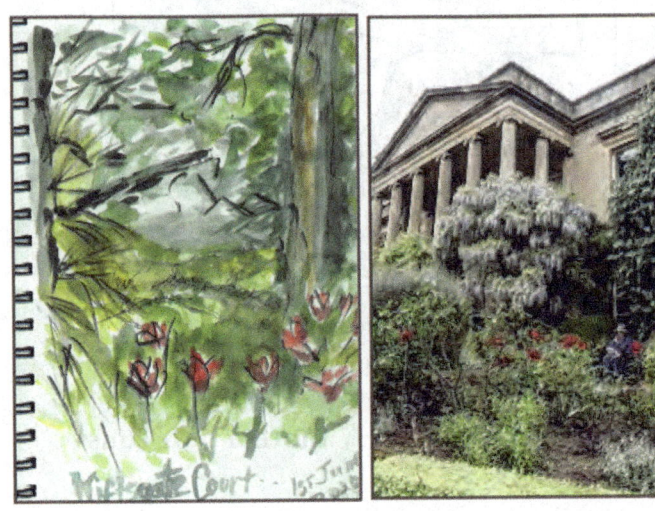

June 18, 2016 - sketchbook note

I've been back home in NH a couple weeks now and am still getting over that "postpartum" I feel after every big adventure. My life in Concord is blessedly quiet but settling back into it takes a while.

June 20, 2016 - Bicentennial Square's bisected rock

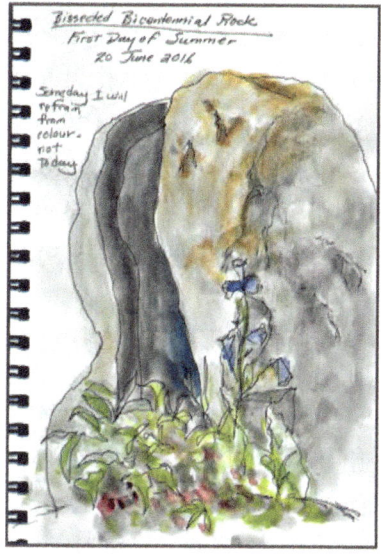

Some days I can refrain from using color—but not today. I love painting rocks.

July 3, 2016

I'm reading Alwyn Crawshaw's book, *The Artist at Work*, and I'm inspired to take notes right here in my sketchbook. He says his purpose in writing an autobiography was to create a kind of map for other artists, and to answer some of those questions that are often asked at his demonstrations. I love the way he writes as much as I enjoy his brilliant watercolors.

I loved when he said, "I think the most precious acquisition [of my life] is the ability to see everyday life as a painting." I remember that minute, a couple years ago, when I was walking down Main Street in Concord, and

I suddenly realized I was "framing the view" with each step, mindlessly designing a composition using what I saw right in front of me. Walking forward felt like a very slow zoom lens. I wondered, "Do film directors and cinematographers have this same way of being in the world, of effortlessly and even compulsively seeing everything as a film set?" I can see how it's a blessing and a curse, to be so easily distracted by every little visual detail of your surroundings.

Crawshaw writes about his years in art trade school, aged 15 to 17, and how self-motivation, even at that early age, is why he got ahead faster than some. He pushed himself.

Crawshaw states one must learn the craft first before experimentation can be any more than a "happy accident" here and there. Just because you're taught how to hold a pencil when you're a child, doesn't mean you have a clue how to draw, right? We all deserve the time it takes to learn.

July 16, 2016 - to Bedrock Garden- Lee, NH

My amazing friend Dana, whom I met through Sketchbook Skool, has become a highly skilled handmade bookbinder, and I was stunned when she gave me a beautiful blank sketchbook that she made using Strathmore Aquarius II paper. I was tempted to save it for something special, but she warned me, "Don't you dare! That book is for sketching!"

So here I am, giving it a go. I did the value sketch first in a separate book made using brown toned paper. I love using grey or brown toned papers with black ink, tint brush, and just a bit of white water-soluble crayon. Next, in Dana's handmade book, using the same design, I took a deep breath and charged right in with that terrifying Pentel brush pen, followed by strong watercolors. What fun! I was so much more confident because I'd done the value study first.

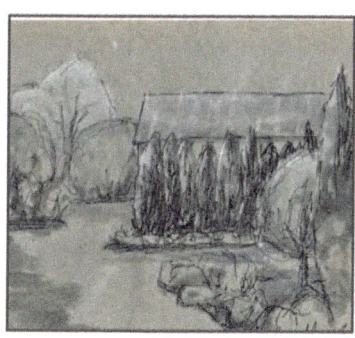 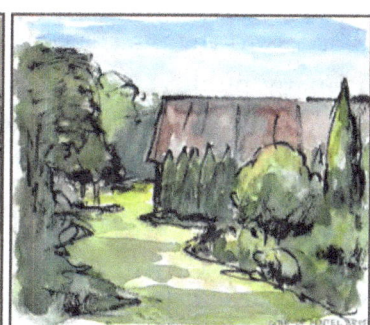

August 13. 2016 - Saturday 4:30pm journal entry

My buddy Dana has convinced me to start a blog. I love to write; I love to talk (my poor friends know that!) but I hate technological learning curves. Nevertheless, Dana promised she'd help with any techno stuff when I hit a snag. (She has her own blog already). I have no more excuses.

But wait, a blog is a step beyond social media belches. It's one step closer to authorship, or at least I think it should be.

Back in the olden days, when Dad worked at Macmillan, there were all these hoops you had to jump through to get more than a handful of carbon copies out into the world. Back then, after careful self-editing, there were actual humans (not apps) who were professional editors! They had studied at length not only spelling and grammar but also style, cohesiveness; those subjective bits that are the underpinning of what makes a sentence sing. Professional editors still exist, of course. Sadly, nowadays, it's also easy to bypass them.

Now, there are rarely any filters at all! All you need is access to the internet, and you can even get that free at many public libraries. Freedom of speech has gone from a chisel and a rock to worldwide blathering by just about anyone.

I'm not saying modern methods are bad, but we've forfeited the Mandatory Pause, that phase between scratching out a rough idea in pencil, and actual publication. Even while I'm manually writing, I sense it could be better, clearer, more honest. Nowadays, there's no mandatory marinade time, no second opinion built into the system. There was no accidental "hit send" back in the days of paper and pencil. Maybe that's why I still like it so much.

We are awash in a sea of first drafts masquerading as polished writing.

Here's the irony: after hinting that I'm sentimental about the good ol' days, I'm joining the mob and starting a blog myself, today. What the heck? And a further irony, in this worldwide web electronic blog, I plan to show people how decades of manual journaling and sketching have given me a healthy way to "keep my thoughts to myself," most of the time, that is.

A handwritten journal is a powerful tool when it becomes a regular friend. You can write in a notebook with a pen or pencil, scribble out all those emotions by letting the natural "fonts" of handwriting emphasize exactly what you mean.

Bear down! Write a single word in screaming capital letters, underline not once like you do on a keyboard, but as many times as you need in order to state, once and for all, that you *really* mean what you're saying. At least for this moment you do.

Let the passions of your head and heart pump all the way down to your fingertip capillaries, where they're released on the page in stark trails of graphite or ink. Ahhh.

Surprisingly, as you see what you're writing, while you're writing it, fresh ideas will come to you that have never occurred to you before. They may not be crystal clear yet, but you keep writing because now you're plugged-in to wisdom and insight that is not yours at all. It's coming *through* you, and you feel like you're merely taking dictation.

You'll be amazed. You will become very protective of your journal with all those twisty meanderings of ink. You've discovered a safe place to keep your embryonic thoughts private, for at least a while. Writing in a journal can release just enough of the internal pressure so we can carry on with our external lives.

Not everything is worth sharing, of course, but many things are worth saying; to yourself first, to try it on for size, at least until the fog clears. Perhaps the only one who needed to hear your words was you. Over time, you'll develop a "whine detector," a vent sensor, and the world will be a better place because of your increasing skills of discernment.

Who, me blog? Yes, but I will never, ever publish the first draft. That's mine, *all mine.*

And the name of it? In honor of my first glimpse of this creative loft apartment, just two years ago today, the blog will be called "Aloft with Inspiration."

August 15, 2016 - small Moleskine sketchbook

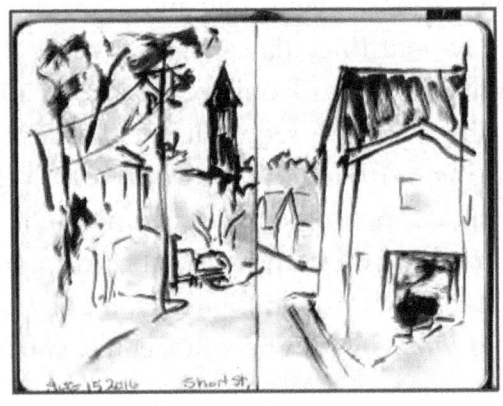

If a Pentel brush pen doesn't stop
your fiddling, nothing will!

September 3, 2016 - journal

I've felt adrift lately, like I'm trying to elbow my way into groups that don't really excite me, but I miss the human contact that was built into having a full-time job. I had this cartoon in my head just now, so I decided it belongs in my journal.

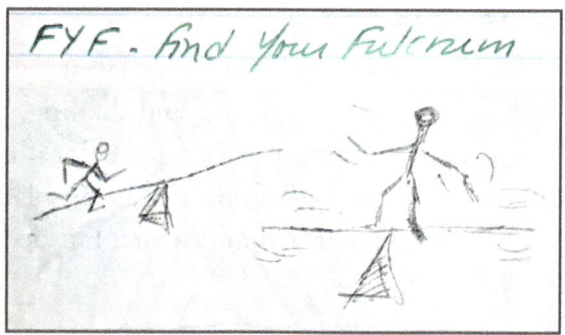

This is all I need: "FYF: Find Your Fulcrum!"

October 5, 2016 - sketchbook note

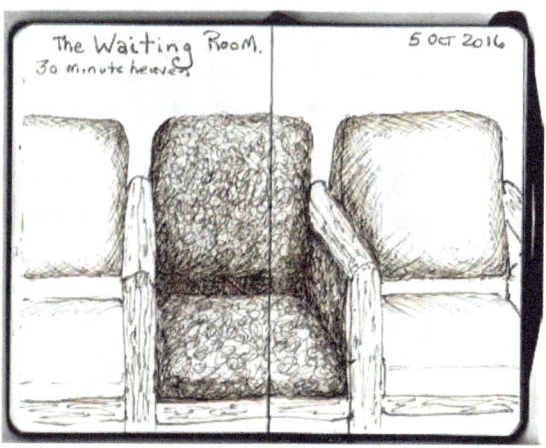

The treatment for one too many tedious doctor's appointments lies in discovering the superpowers of a tiny sketchbook and a brown fine-liner pen. Fully armed, no delay is too long, or too full of dread. Instead, I soar, inspired by upholstery.

October 15, 2016 - 7:30pm

I feel like I've struck gold with this latest collection of tonal sketches: line only, or line and shading, but no color. I'm reveling in the fun of implied color if there is such a thing. My next little book will be all black and white, or perhaps also brown and white, but dedicated to clean, clear values.

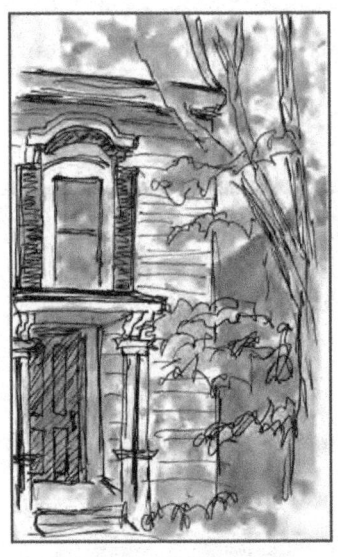

Reminds me of that time Georgia O'Keeffe said she was utterly sick of all her work and was glad she was sick of it. She set aside all her art supplies and went back to charcoal and paper, nothing more. She said she was going to stick with that until she had something to say that she could not say with charcoal. It took a while for her to reach that limit, and my bones are telling me it's now my turn for the same challenge.

October 23, 2016 - 2:30pm

The mums at the Law Enforcement Memorial sculpture were beautiful in the sun today, but the light changes so fast this time of year. Purples and deep burgundies and lemon yellows. This sketch is going in my "B-Plus Sketchbook": black plus one color only. I love how the Lexington Grey ink in my fountain pen looks like pencil marks.

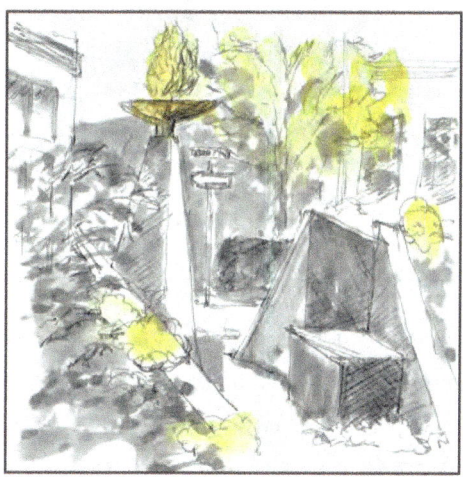

Mini-cyclones of crunchy leaves are dancing and crashing and levitating around me as I sketch, creating sounds like waves breaking on the shore. A recording of this crisp playful sound could be played back during a February blizzard, as a reassurance of hope.

Earlier I noticed the ATM room on the outside of my bank needs raking instead of sweeping! I do love autumn in New England.

November 3, 2016

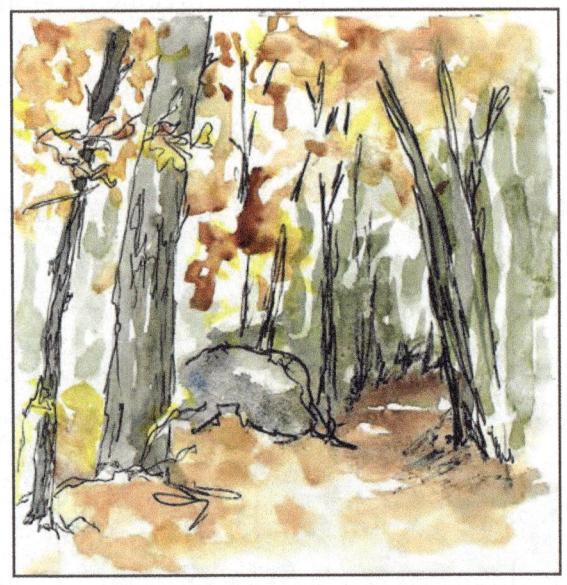

Quick sketching is not my style. Why race to calm down? It never made sense to me. I started this with a bit of ink, then went to my tiny watercolor palette, followed with a bit more line work. It's easier to draw tree trunks if you paint in the foliage first. Who knew? I like the looseness… it's new for me.

November 12, 2016 - At the Currier Museum

I'm so glad I have my sketchbook with me, and that I'm taking notes on this wonderful exhibit entitled, *North Country 1800s*. The paintings are stunning, reminding me of the best English landscape painters, like Constable.

Taking notes at a museum, thumbnail sketches

combined with traditional note-taking, really helps me to see better, to notice things. It's such fun to linger, to first appreciate the overall impression, and then study how the artist created the magic. I see beauty first, yellow ochre second. Studying reflections on water in any painting is ridiculously pleasurable, like peeking behind the curtain at a magic show.

Looking at this painting, I clearly see sheep and cows grazing in a far distant field. But on closer observation, the sheep are merely tiny white dots; the cows are two-color dots. And yet the viewer's mind doesn't hesitate at all. You know the livestock are out to pasture today. That's the magic! Minimal brushwork, maximum illusion. The viewer's mind gets to take part in the pleasure of creation.

Chapter 5: 2017

Early Warning Signs

February 12, 2017

I'm becoming a café hound just so I can take a break and get out with people.

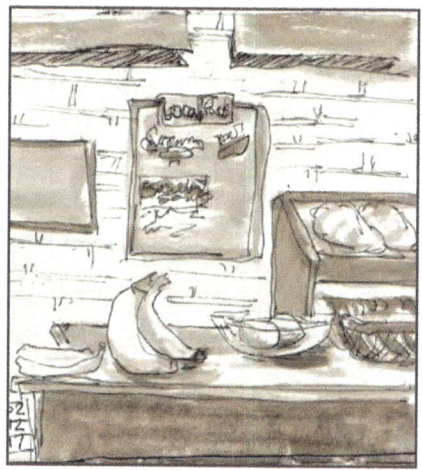

The subconscious search for a tribe of my own is constant even when I'm not aware of it. I can pass for an extrovert, but I find it exhausting. Where do I find kind, creative, quiet people? Perhaps, at this very moment, they're sitting together, contentedly... at the library!

May 14, 2017 - Mother's Day, Red River Theatre

"American Impressionism"- Exhibition-on-Screen series
The interior of a movie theatre before the show starts is visually boring and dimly lit, so I draw my own hand because I have time to kill and an itch to sketch. The theatre is packed, a full house yet again for this wonderful art-film series.

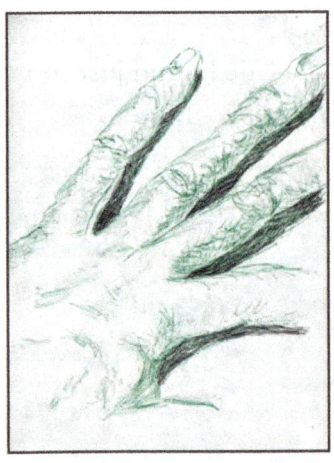

I, Claude Monet is about his inner world more than about his life as a famous artist. He said, "The future seems very black... doubt has overtaken me... I think I am lost." That resonated with me: the drive to create, to draw, to see, to express, to doubt. Monet, Degas, Van Gogh, O'Keeffe all had well-known eyesight problems later in life. It may not have been what drew them to be artists, but if they were anything like me, it brought out the fighter in them, made them dig their heels in and silently declare, "One more painting, damn it; just one more." Luckily, I've had access to medical intervention to extend, perhaps, the time I can see anything at all. Still, there is no cure for this compulsion to look, look again, and take symbolic notes which turn into sketches. I understand the obsession, the relentless drive, even without their talent or skill.

After all, "talent" is just the innate, un-scratchable itch you're born with. "Skill" is what you do about it. "Skill" is the work part.

May 26, 2017

On the verge of Memorial Day weekend, Mom's birthday, and I'm so grateful for her part in my life. That is such a simplification of a complicated relationship.

I realize how fortunate I've been, the nuances of sensitivity I have, simply because of my time with her. She was always gentle with me. She didn't warn me about the harsh realities of life and the bold, aggressive, sometimes angry people I would encounter along the way.

Instead, she gave me a map to the escape hatch of creativity. When she was restless, she knew she needed to create. She looked within for solutions, not to acquisitions. I believe she still had several unfulfilled dreams when she died, but all in all, she did well, especially considering the era in which she lived. My task now (a job that I've given myself, of course), is to die with an empty creativity bucket list, as a way of thanking her for her inspiration and support.

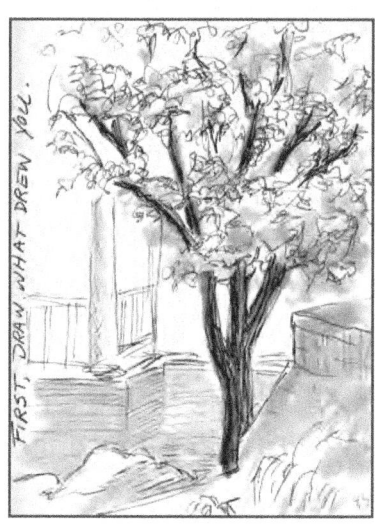

I started this sketch, and an insight arrived: *"First, draw what drew you."* What drew me to look twice was the very black trunk and branches of the tree, darker because they were still wet from the recent rain. The park fountain sculpture is bubbling away, creating a lovely white background noise.

June 3, 2017 - weekend trip to Glebe House in CT with Patrick

What a treat to travel here to admire a Gertrude Jekyll garden, right here in America. Although she never visited this country, she designed three gardens to be created here. This is the only one that survives and is open to the public. The back story is fascinating, the docent at the Glebe House enthusiastic and well informed.

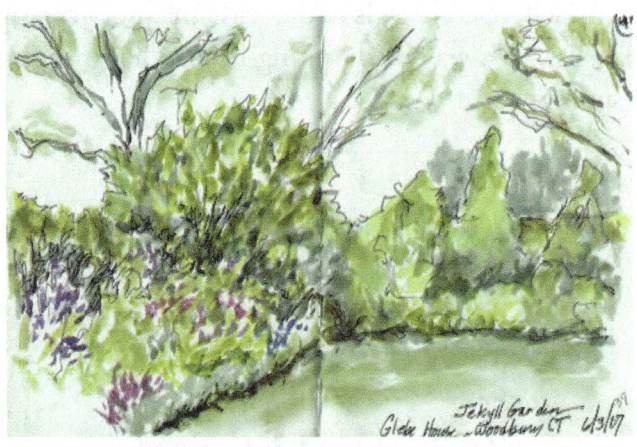

The weather could not be more perfect. The other surprising pleasure is how versatile this inexpensive sketchbook is! It feels natural for writing and drawing, as well as painting.

June 4, 2017 - the next day, Sunday

The central vision in my good eye is suddenly getting weird; I'm not liking this. I'd better call Dr. H. as soon as we get back to Concord. He always says, "Err on the side of caution," and I'm glad he does. I'm so grateful to have my vision care in the hands of doctors I trust, finally! That was not true for a very long time.

June 6, 2017 - Tuesday- after visit to eye doctor

Yes, sure enough, there is a problem. Retinal wrinkles discovered by Dr. H. — tiny vision distortion so far. He said to watch it, and if anything changes, to call back immediately. "Be vigilant but try not to obsess about it." That's the story of the last forty-two years of my life.

July 1, 2017 - three weeks later

Unstable eyesight has brought with it the gift of urgency, and yes, clarity. I made some big decisions, and the relief I feel is extraordinary.

I resigned from membership in an organization that meant a lot to me in the past, but feels different now. I'm also on the verge of resigning from one of my care-provider jobs.

And after those resignations, I am *"re-signing"* a contract with myself. It starts with kindly saying "no thanks" to some friendly social invitations that are lovely, but would inadvertently kick my own creative plans even further down the road. I keep getting the image of being the nice person in the check-out line at the grocery store, who happily lets others go ahead of her because, well, they only have a few items, and well, they look like they're in a rush.

The result being that by the end of the day, many of my heartfelt dreams are still untouched on my to-do list, but now I'm out of energy, saying, "Ah well, there's always tomorrow."

If I learned anything from David's death less than three years ago, and from this recent retinal trouble, it's that there's not always a tomorrow. Every dent in my eyesight is a nudge asking me, "So, Bobb, was there anything else you wanted to do while you can still see, hmmm?"

Resignation feels like liberation. I wonder what will reveal itself once I create the space. I'm sixty-four. It's time.

I've scrambled my whole working life to make ends meet, going from one job to another, but never managing to cobble together anything like a career because I've been paying off medical debts my entire adult life. A moment of lapsed medical insurance would have made both my eyes a "pre-existing condition," so I stayed in dead-end jobs just for the insurance. I couldn't think straight long enough to come up with a better plan, because having an unexpected eye surgery every couple of years simply kicked the hope out of me. I lowered my eyes and my dreams.

In my fifties, I had a brief stint at self-employment, opening a creative arts teaching studio. I loved every minute, except that I lost money on it for the entire seven years. Had it not been for a small inheritance from my blessedly tight-fisted mother, I never would have been able to swing it at all.

And now? I'm coming off yet another set of medical emergencies with my poor little eyeballs and want to consider the possibility that doing much less, at a slower pace, might be just what the doctor ordered.

Slowing down doesn't come naturally. I've been a scrambler from as far back as I can remember. I've worked for forty-five years, and I never caught up with the rabbit of fiscal safety. So, I'm going to sit here at the edge of the racetrack for twelve months and see if the rabbit can run once around the track without me. Some days, bed, a novel, and a cup of tea are the best solution.

July 4, 2017 - Tuesday holiday

My eyesight continues to change; yesterday I was out in bright light, and it took forever for the white-light blindness to disappear once I was back indoors. Very light sensitive, far more than usual. Wearing a hat with a visor, even indoors, seems ridiculous, but that extra shade helps. I can't believe how often these medical emergencies happen on a holiday or on a weekend.

July 7, 2017 - Friday, three days later, trying to calm down

Eyesight now full of black holes, wiggly verticals. I'm in shock. I realize this is *Actually It*. This very moment is what I've subconsciously dreaded since 1975. I lost my left eye in 1992, and now the right one is falling apart. I can't see what I'm writing, it hops in and out, disappearing then reappearing. This is the "Magic Show" that Marie, my good friend with retinitis pigmentosa, has talked about for years. It's heartbreaking and terrifying at the same time.

I can no longer plan my days, and my self-worth, around geographic freedom. Somehow, I have to find freedom within me, without the luxury of car keys or accurate eyesight. I had no idea how often I responded to restlessness by "running an errand," or dropping everything to go visit a friend, or simply taking a joy ride on a beautiful day.

I can still walk, though, and I can breathe, and this life that's been encouraging me to slow down is now forcing me to do so. For better or worse, another adventure begins.

July 8, 2017 - Saturday, a month after the first subtle warning

A full-blown retinal hemorrhage was discovered yesterday, first by me, of course. I knew something was seriously wrong, then my retinal specialist confirmed it.

My mind is racing, thinking of all the things I'll no longer be able to do in this previously spontaneous, self-reliant life I've created over time. No more grabbing the car keys and traveling up to the lake to go sketching for the day because the weather is perfect. No more going to Tarbin Gardens on a whim. No more tiny adventures.

Of course I can get rides. Of course I have friends who are kind and generous. But it's not the same; sketching while someone is glancing at their watch every few minutes is a total waste of time. My solo freedom and independence have always been a big part of my identity. And look at how I'm still assuming that "sketching" will even be an option!

This feels like self-pity, but not entirely. It's summer in New England, finally, and I'm grounded, damn it. Maybe it's not self-pity after all. Maybe it's excruciating grief. It feels like all the stages, all at once. All but acceptance, for now.

Time for a rest and some cucumber slices on my eyelids. This morning's tears remain as huge histamine hangovers this afternoon.

And while I'm up, I may as well chuck all my fine point pens. I had to try three different pens before I found this one that could make a mark fat enough to actually see. Yeah, I'm angry.

July 14, 2017

One week into new distorted vision, is this the new normal or will this be a temporary inconvenience? When even the doctors can't say for sure, then it's up to me how to feel about it, moment to moment, day to day.

Enough! I just decided: I *can* handle this.

Just for today, I can handle what's happening because I still have choices. Even when I can't do a darn thing about my situation, I can always waste time and energy by making matters worse, and I'm choosing not to do that today.

I always have choices.

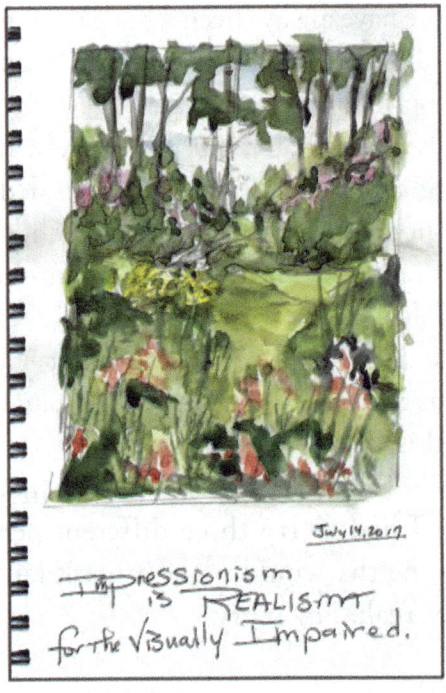

Impressionism is Realism for the Visually Impaired.

The marks that appear on this page may look lovely to others. Only I know that where those marks landed was nowhere near where I was aiming. This is like driving while drunk with dirty glasses, except that I'm wide awake and stone cold sober.

I just kept going, dabbing smears of paint, responding to what I thought was on the page, then making the next mark with the brush.

I literally don't see what other people see when they look at this sketch.

And they can't see what *I* see, even if I'm the only one who knows that.

I see a lovely, fairly meaningless blur.
New world.
Very fuzzy eyesight.
Crystal clear inner vision.

I'll carry on, chin up, even if I have tears streaming down my face.

July 30, 2017 - at Forest Society Conservation Center along the Merrimack River in Concord

In the few weeks since the retinal bleed began, some of the blood has dissipated thanks to several injections of Avastin directly into my eyeball. I can see close-up shapes a bit more clearly. I'm guessing at what the people on the beach look like, but thankfully, I can see my blurry sketchbook a little better than I could three weeks ago.

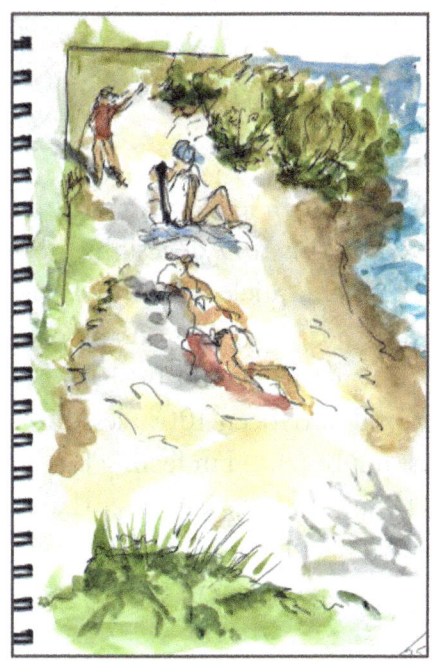

I'm at a secret little beach where I'm luxuriating up on the hill in the dappled shade. Two dogs appear to be running a motocross race through the various obstacles of blankets and half-naked men and women. Despite it being the height of summer, the sky is the most glorious shade of September-blue, no humidity, and just enough puffy little clouds to give you a sense of distance.

August 2, 2017 - Penacook

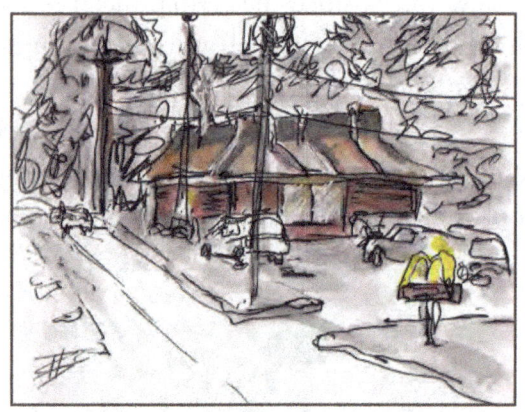

It's fun to learn I can lean on a guardrail waiting for the bus and enjoy this fuzzy eyesight, no need to "get it right" when I do a quick sketch. If I had a table and seat and were taking my glasses on and off and fiddling a lot more, this picture would be 10% better, but the experience would have been 100% less fun. I'm making bolder marks, not because I'm feeling bold or confident, but because I can't see lines any finer than this!

How funny, when you don't see well, your bold sketches look like you knew exactly what you were doing. What a great disguise! All drawing is simplification and interpretation. Mine is just moreso!

August 11, 2017 - Friday morning

I volunteered at a local senior center this morning, and no one showed up. There I sat, with my sketchbook, didn't feel like writing, but I noticed there was a little collection of glass bottles on the side table, so I decided to draw them. The arrangement was uninspiring, so I drew four rough blocks and sketched partial vignettes instead.

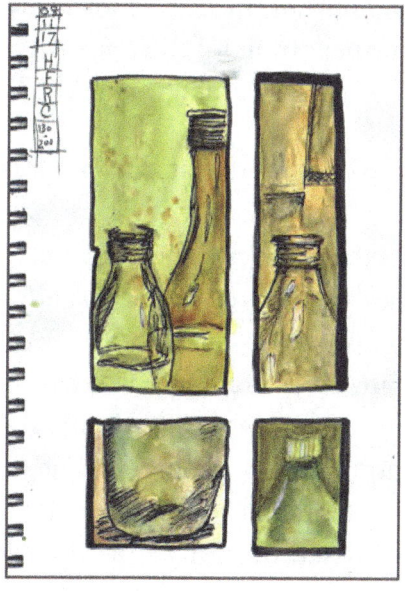

I sense I'm here on the planet to help people learn how to access a peaceful moment any time throughout the day, just like I did instinctively by creating those four sketches instead of getting annoyed that people didn't show up for my class. I have so much experience "triaging" the rough patches that life hands us.

I learned years ago that sometimes, all I need is a pleasant interruption, not a cure. The discouragement I've felt so often is really not clinical depression; it's simply a hopeless thought repeating over and over. An engaging interruption, like sketching, airlifts me out of the muck and is like a reset button. There's no cure for the human condition, but there are some delightful treatments!

It's time for me to revisit the wisdom of Misao Jo, Pema Chodron, Huston Smith, Taro Gold, Robert Henri, Henry David Thoreau. I can be content with these true hearts until my next train (of thought) arrives. As my bro David used to say, "Onward Through the Fog!"

August 11, 2017 - later that day, at Bicentennial Square

I've been scrounging around for an art class to join, and I just heard a voice inside me casually whisper, "Ya know, Bobbie, you *could* teach it..."

Now my mind is racing, yes! I can call it "Look at That!" and teach exactly what's missing from every art course and book I've ever seen. The *joy* is so much more important than the technique! I can teach fun, just like Gif Russell did for us in 1986. Find the one thing they're doing right, then tell them all about it. There's no room for an Inner Critic — we're playing! And I know where I want to do it. Kimball Jenkins School of Art, right here in Concord.

I'm scribbling loose ideas as fast as I can; thought bubbles, mind maps, hearing that voice say, "Why not, why not?" over and over again. I know I know too much; don't scare the beginners who are already nervous. Distill, distill…

I feel like a renegade; I want to teach the honoring of intuition, not obedience to authority or technique. Joy, not perfection. Sure, I'll demonstrate a bit of technique, just so they don't stumble too much, but the rest is pure adventure. And it must be affordable, one class at a time; no need to force people to shell out over a hundred dollars just to see if they like it. Affordable sketching for anyone and everyone who wants to give it a go. Now *that's* revolution!

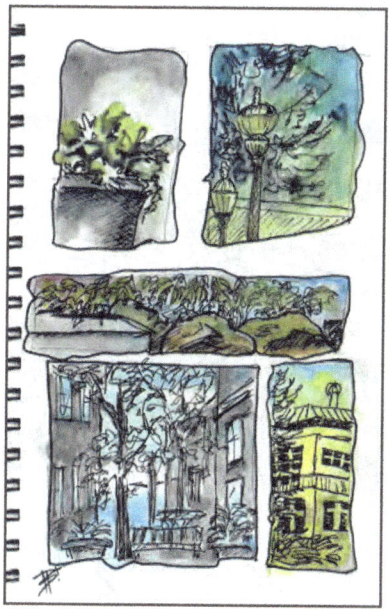

It's an insane coincidence that today is the three-year anniversary of moving to my beautiful loft apartment, right here in the building behind me. And only one year ago this week, I started my blog. Early August is apparently a fertile time.

My biggest challenge is that I want to write and sketch simultaneously. What a cool problem!

Outside the café, Bicentennial Square: this blue green collection of sketches is a reflection of how randomly excited I feel!

August 22, 2017 - Tuesday

I got the gig! My pitch to Kimball Jenkins School of Art worked! The first class will be six weeks from now, on October 7th, 10am to 12 noon. If I can help enhance the creative community in Concord, push the door open so just a few more wannabes will dare to step in with us, I'll feel like it was a success.

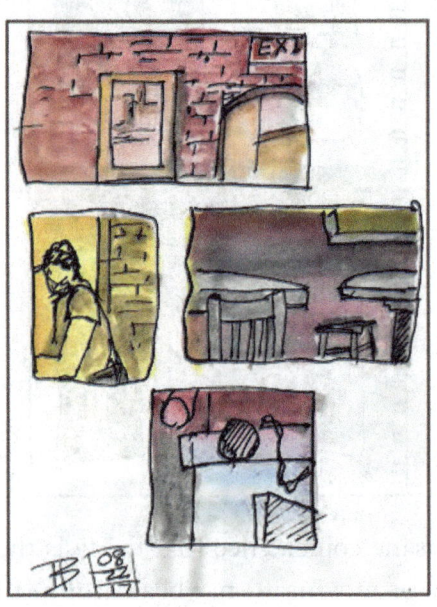

Sometimes this cursed low vision feels like just the kick in the butt that I need. (When did this knee-jerk instinct of turning lemons into lemonade start? Probably about the time I got sick of listening to my own whining!)

I just drew a few squares with bold, waterproof pen on this page, and throughout the day I've filled them with fat-lined, simple drawings. Then I topped them all with rich, juicy watercolor washes and voila! No pussyfooting around here!

My whole life feels like one big experiment. The sketching might as well be too.

August 26, 2017 - four days later

My mind continues to race with all sorts of ideas for a lesson plan for the class. How to distill forty years of sketching and painting experience into a two-hour class, and include a few golden nuggets from my mentors as well? I've uncovered a core question to ask them, with multiple choice answers:

Why bother sketching?
Answers:

A. You'll get a time-out from your head.
B. Others will assume you know what you are doing because you are looking at stuff.
C. You will learn how to BREATHE and not interrupt your sketch.

D. Your powers of observation will improve effortlessly.
E. Eventually your eyes and hand will be introduced to each other.
F. The best answer is, "all of the above," of course.

Right now, I know I'm far more invested in promoting this class than the school is (I'm a relative unknown to them), so I'd better do a lot of the marketing. I created a poster to hang in local cafes, markets, and on community bulletin boards.

I've decided to call the class, *"Look at That! Seeing through Sketching."* That was the point from the beginning. *"Sharpen your eyesight to open your heart."*

August 28, 2017 - later the same day

My eye was just dilated before yet another injection, so I can see even less than usual, and it will be a while before my ride arrives, so here I sit on the bench outside. I must be crazy or "sketch-addicted" but I have this intense need to draw, to take notes on what I can barely see. It's my way of fidgeting. As usual, what ends up on the paper is much sharper than what I can see. I'm using the Pilot G-2 /10 pen (which has water-soluble ink) because it's bold, otherwise I couldn't even see the marks I've put down. If my ride takes much longer, I'll have time to soften the lines a bit with my water brush.

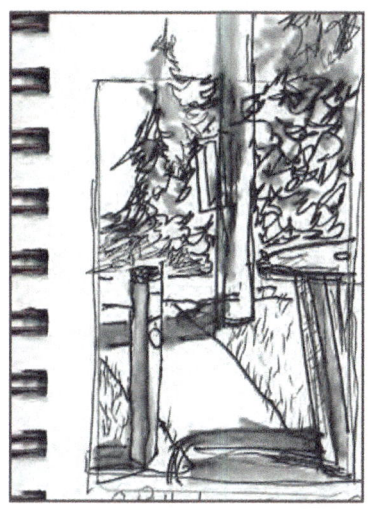

I'm sure few people can imagine how comforting it is to have these tools (a sketchbook and a pen) resting in my hands, even when I can't clearly see what I'm doing. These tools are my best and most loyal friends. Simply holding them calms me somehow.

August 30, 2017 - Little Harbor, Cohasset MA with Carra

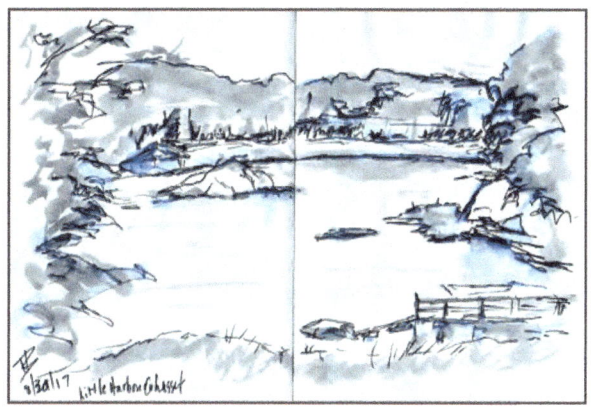

What a delight to be here. I'm sitting on the deck overlooking the harbor, and despite having all my art supply toys with me, I started with a simple Flair felt tip for the drawing and follow it with plain water brush work to make the black lines bleed a bit. It's only then that you see the black ink is really a lovely blue-black. When that was finished, I still felt something was missing, so I added grey tint-brush masses here and there. This'll be a fond memory when I look back on it in years to come.

August 30, 2017 - Boston Common, later that day

My niece Carra and her friend Joanna have been gracious enough to be volunteer art students today so I can try out my lesson plans for the upcoming class. We started in Joanna's apartment, introducing these wonderful women to their simple art supplies, then we got on the T and made our way to Boston Public Garden.

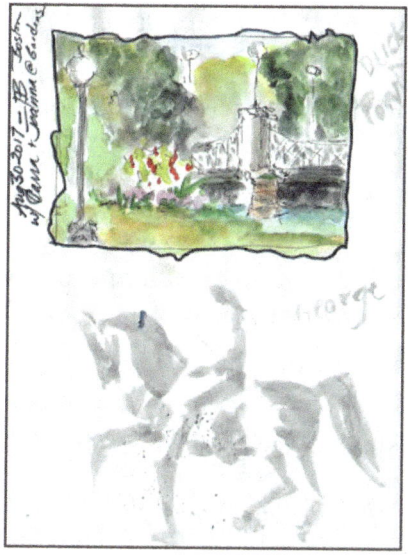

I had to find a way for us to sit in the shade because my eye is still so light sensitive. We finally found a spot, and I started on the bottom of the page with a "shadows only" quick sketch of the statue of George Washington. No line work at all, just grey tint-brush painting of the abstract deep shadow areas and let the viewer's eye do the rest of the work. Next, I attempted that pond and bridge scene in the distance, but I had so much trouble seeing that far that a lot of it was guesswork. The result may be pleasing, but the effort was less enjoyable.

Note to Self: *Only Sketch What You Can Easily See!*

September 9, 2017

Finally, I was able to pass the DMV vision test, so I can drive again after 63 days and several eye injections of Avastin. Cautiously optimistic.

September 13, 2017 - a very special new beginning

I started doing the exercises in the workbook, *Getting Your Important Work Done,* which I downloaded from Michael Nobbs' *Go Gently.co* website in Wales.

Here's my first mission statement: "As long as I have eyesight, I can write and sketch and paint. These will fill my heart and will attract opportunities." That's underlined here in my sketchbook; it's my new North Star for now.

Here's a valuable question from Michael's workbook:

"If I didn't have to do it perfectly, I would…"

- Work bigger in watercolor.
- Write an illustrated book.
- Have prints available. Paintings, ink sketches.
- Write essays, maybe a memoir.

We shall see…so to speak!

September 16, 2017

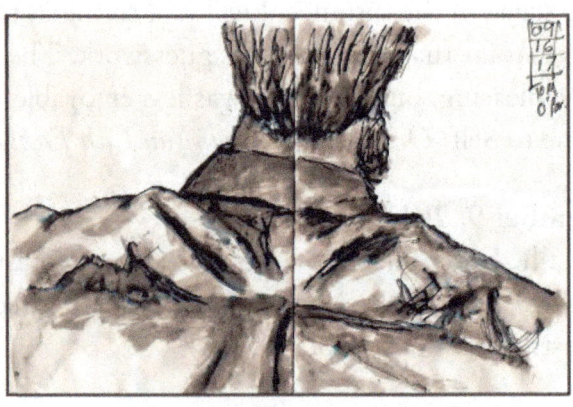

I'm continuing to realize that the less I can see, the bolder my artwork is. My self-confidence is so fragile, and my artwork is hollering, just so I can see it. The irony never ends.

September 27, 2017 - notes in 3.5 by 5-inch spiral sketchbook

Less than three weeks back driving my car, and I'm still finding "every site a treat for sight." I wonder how many people have parked here and not even noticed this lovely fence?

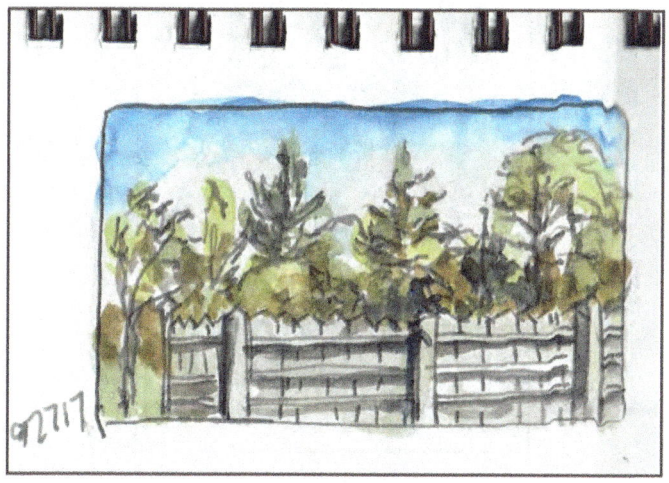

Using a tiny sketchbook like this one can be challenging. The best way for me to maximize its usefulness is to place a standard business card on the page, then trace around it, thus creating a framed area on the page in which to draw. I enjoyed doing this little sketch while I was waiting for an appointment (I have the habit of arriving early to everything now, for just this reason.)

September 29, 2017

It's hard to explain to people that how I draw is not how I see. With poor eyesight, when I look at a crisp image, it's not crisp for me at all, even if the marks I make on the page are sharp and clear. When I look at a blurry image, it's even blurrier for me than it is for others.

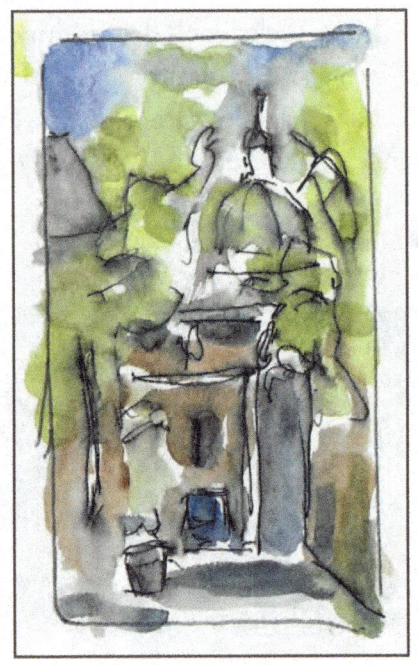

In this sketch today, the ink lines bled more than I expected, because I thought I was using a permanent pen, but I wasn't. The result is, I think this may be more like how I see, nothing distinct at a distance, wobbly lines everywhere. When I hold something six inches from my nose, I can see part of it fairly well, in just one eye. Thank goodness for that.

October 5, 2017 - two days to go until the first art class

It's funny the looks you get when you're sitting in an alleyway on a curbstone that probably has supported a few drifters throughout the decades. Instead… you're sketching! I have to laugh; people see me drawing something, then look over to see what on earth I'm looking at that's worthy of a sketch. Then they shrug, smile, and walk away.

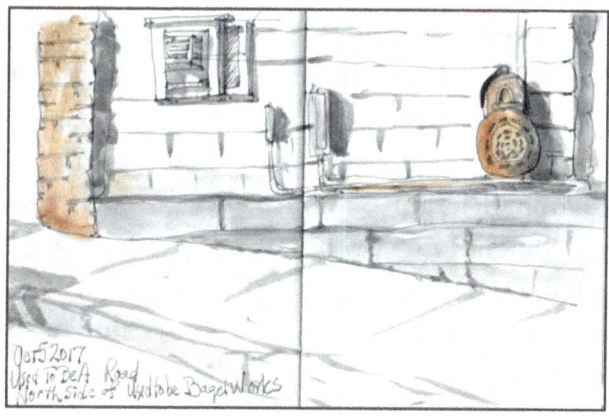

There's beauty everywhere if you have eyes like mine.

October 7, 2017 - my art class begins!

Today was my first class at Kimball Jenkins. Lovely people attended, good turnout. I was a wreck; tried to cover way too much material. I'm learning. Eight students, mix of cautious, nervous, shy, and confident. Their faces reflected all the emotions I was feeling as the instructor. I over-delivered, interrupted myself repeatedly. Bad idea to try to tell them everything I've learned in the last three decades during one two-hour class. Time to tweak the lesson plan!

I intentionally wanted to offer this as a "one-off" to make it affordable, and less of a commitment. Now I see there may be a need for a series; there's so much to teach and learn.

October 23, 2017

These creative circle planning sessions are really making a difference. I see my restlessness is a symptom of having no gentle discipline that keeps me on course, no North Star. Without a family, any long-term sense of purpose can be elusive.

I was just offered a chance to teach four more classes at Kimball Jenkins, and slowly I'm seeing this trajectory come into focus. Funny, it's so un-American to intentionally not be setting goals. Instead, I'm setting a course, a trajectory, and what appears along the way, will be the logical result. Faith comes in so many forms, doesn't it?

I like the idea of a monthly theme, rather than a monthly goal. Far less pressure, more guidance; gentle pull rather than a shove. A North Star, rather than a Taser.

November 11, 2017

"I can't see that far." I say that so often when I'm out sketching with someone, as they point out something interesting to me. They see what ends up in my sketchbook and think I'm using great restraint to leave out a lot of unnecessary details. In truth, I can't even see the

details. It's ironic that I suppose my sketches look "even better nowadays" to some people because of my diminished eyesight.

I walk slowly, I see slowly, and drive as little as possible. I passed the vision test for my driver's license, but ever since that mini-hemorrhage in my good eye, I'm scared to drive. My entire life needs to slow down, and I hope my personal desperation isn't leaking out into my art class too much. I'm passionate about inspiring people to really see, really look at things. I sense though, on some days, there's a bit of "vision jealousy" underneath all my enthusiasm.

November 14, 2017

I just saw *Loving Vincent* at the theatre, and halfway through it I realized I must go to watch it at least one more time. The entire film is an assemblage of paintings. Over 100 artists created over 65,000 paintings, all brilliantly strung together to create a feature-length animated film. I'm so glad I was there alone and was alone afterward. I was so touched; it was a powerful experience.

It feels like, perhaps, the ending of the film was the point. A life well-lived, for only a while, is sometimes enough. The fight with chronic poverty, and frequent discouragement, can be overwhelming, a spirit-breaker. Even a deal-breaker.

December 26, 2017 - sketchbook work

I love working plein-air, on site, with all the wind and heat and bugs and all those other irritants. But in the dead of winter, working from a summery photo is therapeutic.

For the time I was sketching this little scene, I felt I was sitting there in the strong August sun.

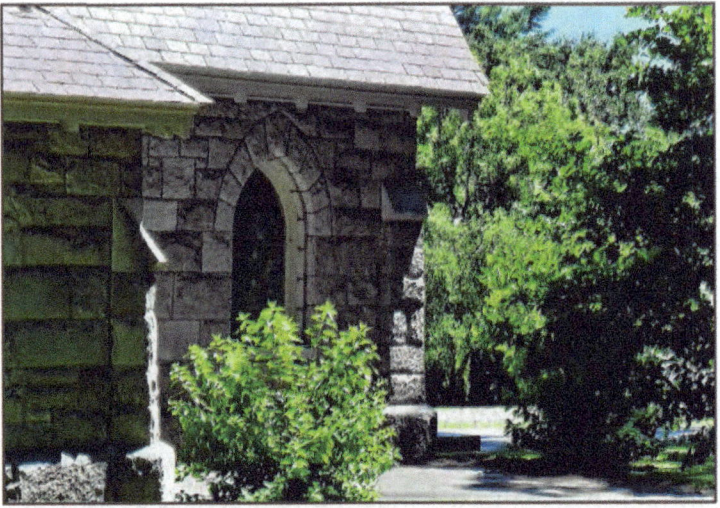

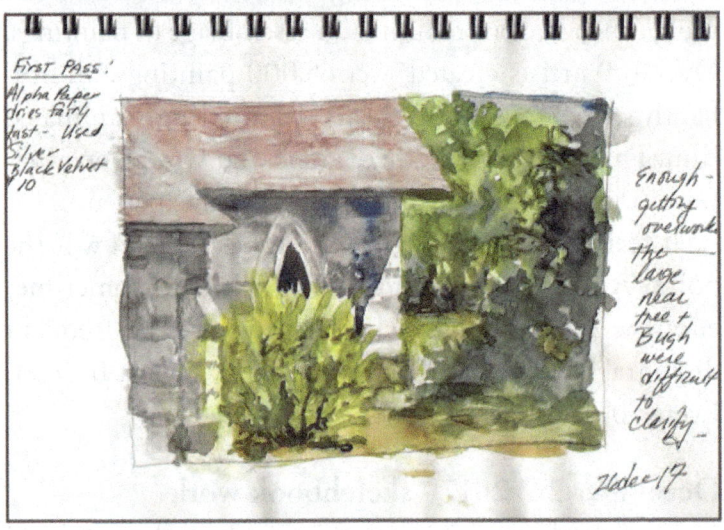

As always, that rich shadow cast by the roof eave made the whole painting pop.

Chapter 6: 2018

A Sisyphus Year

January 3, 2018 - Strathmore 400 series watercolor sketchbook

This watercolor paper is okay, but it's going to take some getting used to. It's made of wood pulp, not 100% cotton/rag, and it makes such a difference in how it behaves. The graded wash in the sky was difficult to do, the absorbency of the paper varied so much. I felt I even had to scrub the paint on at times.

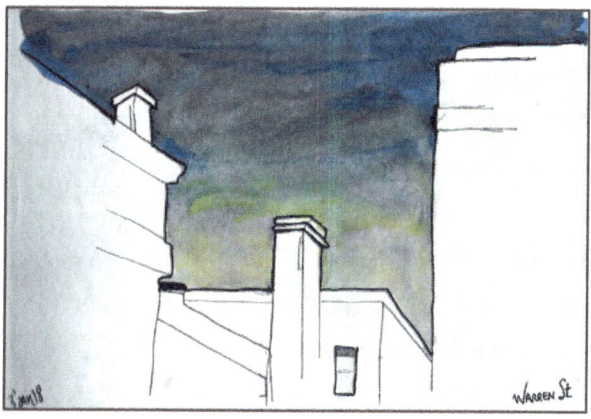

This is all best kept to myself though; that is, unless I'm teaching. When people admire my artwork, there's no need to tell them how frustrating the process was. That is, unless they also paint in watercolor, in which case they might well already know! It would be like a wedding planner telling people at the reception what a nightmare the bridal party was! Only other event planners (and artists) know that the compliments are proof that you made it look effortless.

Jan 22, 2018

Another small retinal bleed happened on January 5th and because of it, I decided today to take that trip to Scotland in June while I can still see. Bought plane tickets just now. My logic may only make sense to me; It feels like the clock is ticking loudly.

February 11, 2018 - good friends' kitchen

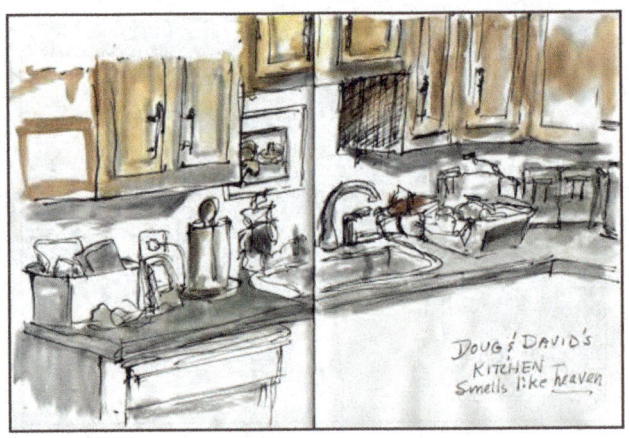

The best way to stay out of the way when visiting friends who are wonderful cooks is to snuggle up at their breakfast table and sketch away. D & D are a blur of activity, so as always, I'm better at sketching inanimate objects.

March 23, 2018

My brain keeps wandering back to thinking about writing a memoir, maybe just for myself, to make some sense of this strange life of mine. Thinking in cartoons clarifies everything.

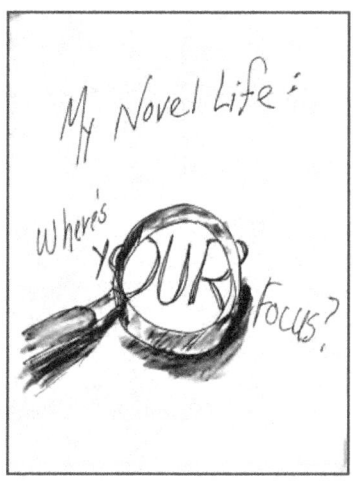

March 24, 2018 - March for Our Lives at NH State House

After the Parkland shooting in Florida last month, the rally against gun violence happened today in Washington, DC and in cities around the country. I got choked up at the strange blend of anger and powerlessness I sensed in the crowd. Many of us feel our beautiful country has been hijacked.

The speeches were inspiring, the diversity in the crowd encouraging: students, young families, elders; down ski parkas and woolen coats next to people wearing barn jackets. All of one mind, wondering what it's going to take to stop the madness.

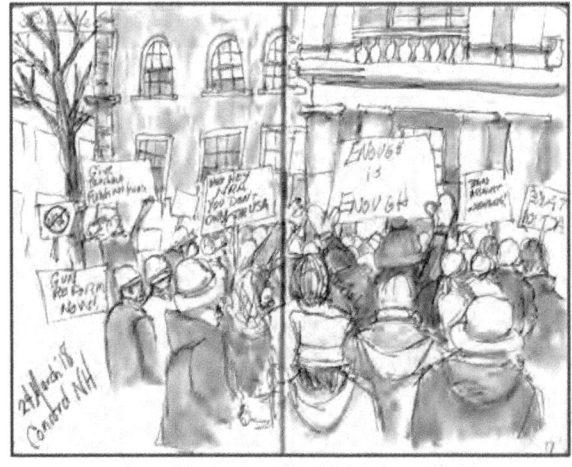

I found a spot beside the statue of Daniel Webster and was glad I'd brought my pen-pouch necklace and sketchbook. It was crowded, strangers standing elbow to elbow, and I realized while doing this sketch that although my arms were pressed tight by my sides, I still could sketch with full access to different pens and my tint brush, thanks to that pen-pouch necklace. Maybe I could create pouches like this myself. I bought this one from my Japanese Saori weaving teacher back in 2005. It would be fun to weave and sew a few of these pouches for my students to use. We shall see.

April 21, 2018 - Saturday morning

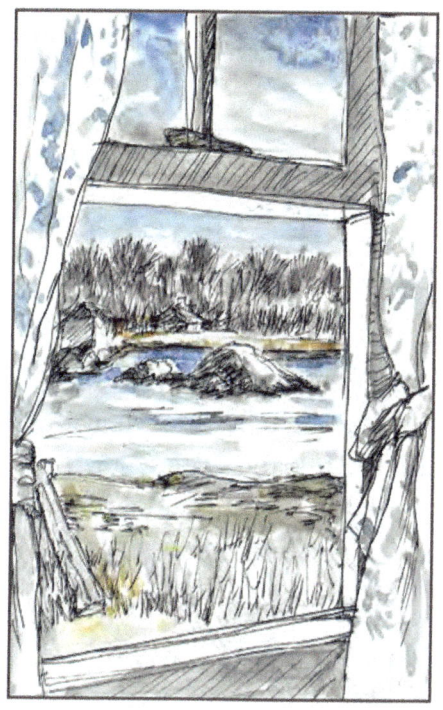

The best part of waking early when you're a guest in someone's house is you get to gaze out the bedroom window and capture the gentle breezes ruffling the curtains. Now that view is mine forever.

May 1, 2018

Using my original Cotman palette and fine point Lamy pen. Thinking of page design while loving the coffee and oatmeal raisin cookie, which never stood a chance of being included in the sketch, of course!

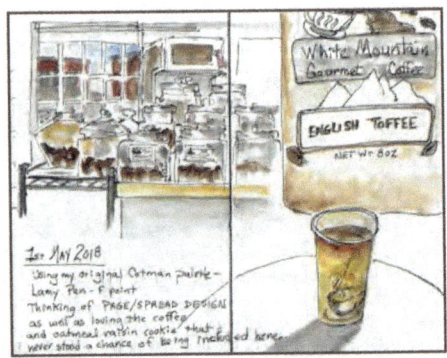

May 2, 2018 - Wednesday afternoon

I did this pencil sketch a month ago and went back today to finish the ink and watercolor. The interruption a month ago was well worth it. I have to write down the story to be sure I remember it.

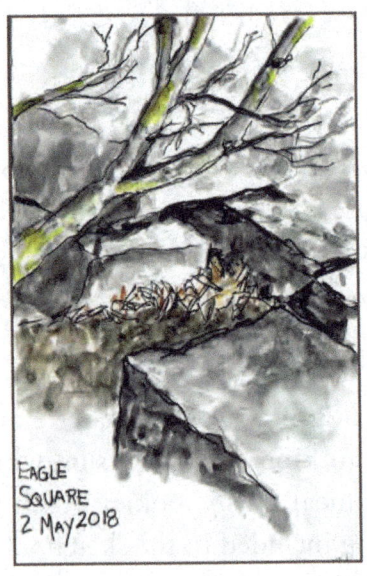

April 2nd was one of the first sunny warm days this year, finally free of icy patches on the sidewalks. I scouted out a good place to sit outside to draw and ended up in Eagle Square, next to the granite-block mound that becomes a waterfall fountain in the summer. As I was sketching, a clean-cut young man walked down several steps past where I was sitting, set down his backpack, and pulled out his cell phone.

Many minutes later, I looked up at the same time he glanced over. He smiled, and quietly said, "Excuse me, do you mind if I look at your drawing?"

I said, "Not at all," so he walked back up the steps to where I was sitting.

He was shy but friendly and started telling me about his artistic 15-year-old daughter, and how she would love to see what I was doing. After a while, he asked if he could sit down. His politeness impressed me. It's a public park, after all, and I appreciated his gentlemanly behavior.

In the next two full hours, Jasen, this charming forty-year-old man ("100% Polish," he grinningly told me), recounted his life story and asked for nothing in return but a sincere conversation. We took turns being captivated by what the other one had to say. He brought out the very best in me, the part that felt it could afford to be positive and generous toward a total stranger. He treated me like a wise woman, and I'm so glad I took the time to listen to another human being whom I'll probably never meet again.

At the end of our conversation, without a drop of self-pity, he acknowledged he was homeless, but that he knew things would get better soon. When we parted, I asked, "Is a hug okay?" and he beamed. "Of course, wow, thanks."

I went back today, a month later, to finish the sketch. It was another sunny day, and I half expected to see him there, two specters returning through a rare portal in time. I took a deep breath, smiled, pulled out my art kit and said thanks to the spirit of Serendipity. You meet the nicest people while urban sketching.

May 3, 2018

My favorite woodland sights this time of year are the stubborn old beech leaves, sun-bleached and brittle, yet clinging to their branches, refusing to fall until evicted by this year's new buds.

I tried out my new trekking poles today and find them very helpful for balance, especially with my questionable vision. Excellent investment. Also, I've added "Yaya" brand earth-friendly bug spray to my art kit, made right here in Contoocook, NH. The ingredients are almost perfume for me: citronella, clove, cedarwood, peppermint, rosemary. And yes, the bugs hate it! Win-win!

May 25, 2018 - Bicentennial Square, where else?

I wonder what sort of calligraphic ink marks are effective for a huge patch of lacy springtime tree leaves. There must be marks that are suggestive, yet not fussy. I'll have to check out some of my mentors' work online. This spot color seems to work well enough.

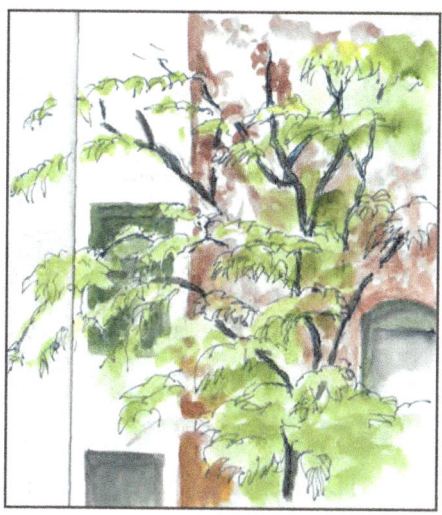

It felt good to add the window and door to the whitewashed building at the last minute.

May 29, 2018

Learned today about the new art classes that Ryan Linehan, the interim director at Kimball Jenkins, wants to offer to young addicts in recovery, and I got very excited. The *Concord Monitor* will do a story and photo shoot to help promote it. I hope I can be a part of this effort. I can identify with the despair those kids have often felt, and I have some tools, including a sketchbook, that I've used to deal with my own emotional challenges.

June 8, 2018 - a beautiful Friday afternoon

Really enjoyable session with Maddie this afternoon, the photographer with the *Concord Monitor*. The article will most likely be in next week's paper. Life is so good.

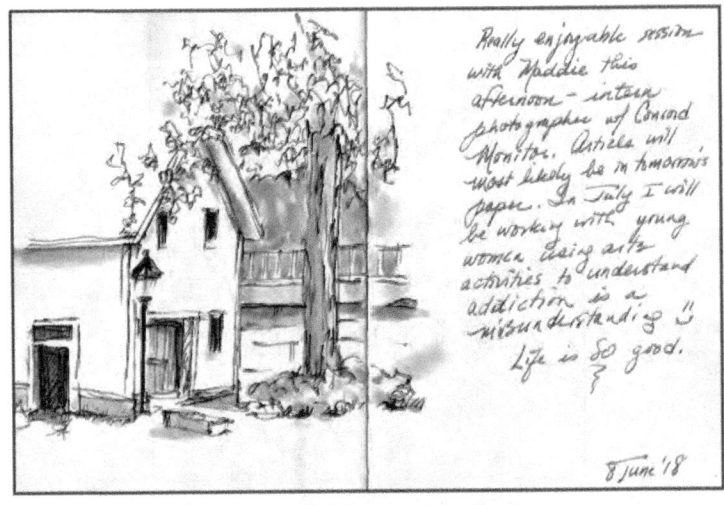

June 11, 2018 - Monday morning

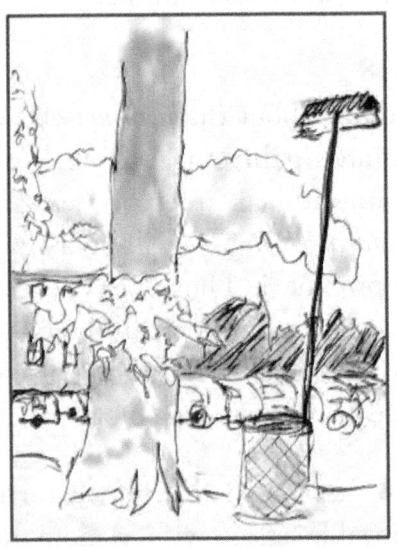

8:30am. appointment with the retina specialist for unexpected 4th retinal shot in 11 months. I'm sketching anyway while I wait for the taxi — can't really see what I'm drawing or writing — eye still dilated and distorted from retinal injection.

Later, same memorable day

Noontime, just got the newspaper. A picture of me sketching on the steps of the Kimball Jenkins mansion is on the cover of the *Concord Monitor*, along with a story about the recovery art classes the School will be offering. This program is part of a grant paid for by the parents of a local 19-year-old artistic woman who died of a heroin overdose. I'm eager to work with these young folks.

2:30pm - opening the door at the laundromat, I sprained my right pinkie finger. Loud cracking noise. X-rays say it's a bad sprain. May not write or draw much for a week or so.

Note to self: Poor eyesight is hazardous for the rest of your body too!

June 14, 2018 - sketchbook notes

I feel like Dorothy clicking my ruby slippers together, saying, "I DO believe I'll be okay, I-do-I-do-I-do…"

I suppose it sounds crazy to get on a plane five days from now, having just had yet another small eye bleed three days ago. I've put my life on hold so many times since 1975, postponing dreams, because I'm never sure when I'll have my next emergency trip to an operating room. No more.

The doctor knows I'm booked for this trip to Scotland. I asked if he had an opinion about it, and although he didn't give me any real advice, he showed no alarm. He seems to understand the long road I've been on my entire adult life. I think he knows that if there's something I want to travel to see, I'd better get to it sooner rather than later.

So, now to the packing prep! Selecting a sketchbook for a trip is such fun—so many sizes and types of paper, pros and cons everywhere. I landed on this 6 by 8-inch hardcover book, 80 sheets. It's inexpensive yet has decent paper. I know I'll be taping / collaging pieces of paper in here, ticket stubs, etc., and I'll want to do a lot of writing, list-making, and random scribbling of ideas too. A sketchbook made of precious 140lb. cold-press watercolor paper would be a waste. I'll take a few small single sheets of good watercolor paper with a clipboard too, so if I have the time, I can do a "real" watercolor.

Things to Buy: waterproof walking boots, midge-proof head covering.

Things to Do: notify bank and post office and get temporary international coverage on my cellphone. Also, calm down, just a tad!

June 19, 2018 - Tuesday, 11:30am in Boston, Logan Airport

And so it begins. I've eaten my first airport sandwich; a tuna wrap I will no doubt be tasting until tomorrow. The plane won't even begin boarding until two hours from now, so there's plenty of time to indulge in Wi-Fi, reading, fidgeting, and sketching.

I have a perverse affection for airport waiting areas,

bus terminals, any place where total strangers are busy maintaining their separate realities while sitting in close quarters.

A slow-moving Southwest Airlines plane just passed near the terminal window. The tail end looked like a shark-fin slowly gliding past the heads of the preoccupied seated passengers in this waiting area of Terminal A. I'm the only one who noticed, so I'm quietly humming the *Jaws* movie theme, smiling.

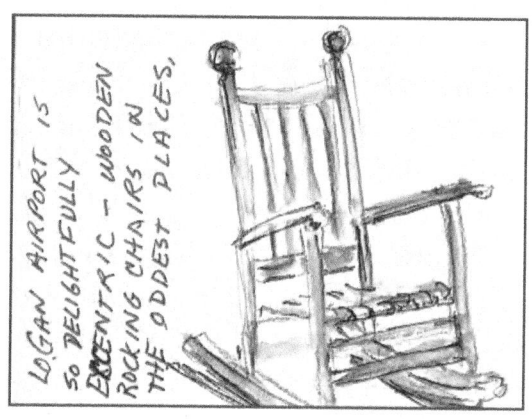

LOGAN AIRPORT IS SO DELIGHTFULLY EXCENTRIC — WOODEN ROCKING CHAIRS IN THE ODDEST PLACES.

Leave it to Boston's Logan airport to provide white rocking chairs where the view of planes taking off and landing is clear. The chairs remind me of JFK, fondly. I understand Charlotte NC and Philadelphia provide strategically placed rocking chairs too.

June 20, 2018 - at the hotel in Glasgow, Scotland

I'm so glad I made plans to arrive two full days before my Road Scholar traveling companions get here. I'll have time to sleep and rest as much as I like and with any extra energy, I can wander around a little and pretend that navigating in a foreign country, with occasional language challenges, is perfectly normal for me, ha! For today, trips back and forth to the restaurant right here in the hotel are enough. Ahh, jetlag and sleep.

June 21, 2018 - Thursday, 5pm and happily tired

Slept well, and was raring to go this morning, thank goodness! I walked much farther than I expected to get from the bus stop in town to the Kelvingrove Museum. What a stunning building. The Baroque architecture is ornate, the art collection stunning. The real shock happened when I was walking around in the upper gallery. I suddenly heard live organ music, thanks to the daily recitals on the Kelvingrove pipe organ. This massive organ was commissioned in 1901, has 2,889 organ pipes (!), and because it's not situated in a cathedral, the music played included secular as well as sacred, thoroughly delightful. I'm so glad I didn't know about it in advance; what a surprise!

The following day, June 22nd Friday midday

My Road Scholar traveling companions will arrive later today, but for now, I'm off on an adventure in Glasgow proper. Bus to the Buchanan Subway stop, no idea how to use the subway pass (it's not like Boston), so I'm "drafting" instead, following along behind people who look like they know what they're doing. When in doubt, blend in, build in extra time. I could ask for help, but I also like the "watch-and-learn" approach.

Ultimate destination: Glasgow Botanical Gardens. Free Admission: that certainly shows wise cultural priorities!

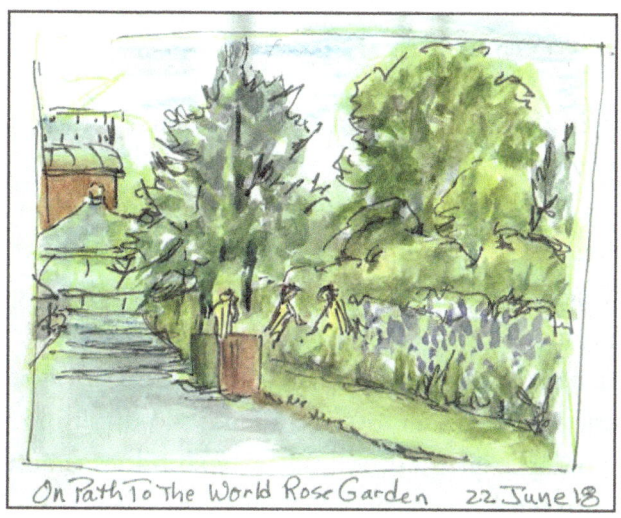

On Path To The World Rose Garden   22 June 18

I did this sketch while sitting on the path to the World Rose Garden, admiring lovely purple flowers all along the border. I can't really see any of the detail from here, other than the garden volunteers in their yellow outfits, working away, clearly knowing what they're doing. They remind me of worker bees.

Traveling alone is Introverts' Nirvana. I haven't spoken more than monosyllables since I left New Hampshire, except for necessities with hotel and restaurant staff. Eavesdropping is fun but Americans often make me cringe. Too loud, too often.

As far as I know, today (a Friday) is not a holiday, and yet there are so many young families here at the Gardens, including dads. So healthy.

The rest of my companions will be at the hotel soon, so it's time to head back by subway and bus. I'm unreasonably comfortable wandering around this no-longer-foreign city.

June 23, 2018 - Saturday, Aigas Field Centre, Beauly Scotland

I've met Lady Lucy and Sir John Lister-Kaye, lovely people. I read a couple of Sir John's books before I arrived here, and I love his writing style, expressive and humorous.

At one point in his talk, he was explaining to us Americans what a "croft" is: a small landholding with landholders' rights, although the tenant doesn't actually own the land. He explained, "It's really very simple; a croft is an area of land completely surrounded by regulations." He was skilled at telling tales to draw us in, fostering a fresh interest in subjects many of us knew very little about. The local natural history is fascinating.

June 25, 2018 - Monday, taking a pause

I've taken so many photographs, endless gorgeous vistas, and haven't felt like I had the time to settle into my slow way of sketching. Sketching is meditative for me, and this trip has been far more stimulating than I expected. Next stop: Cawdor Castle.

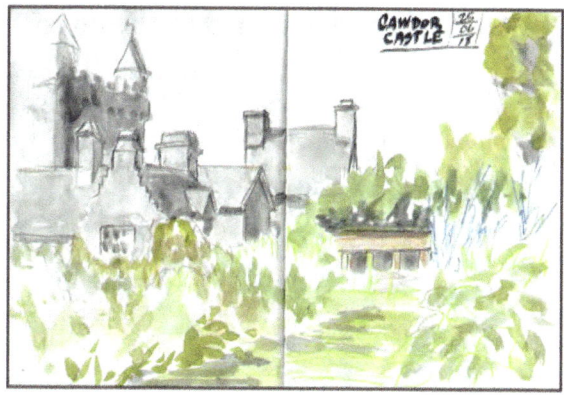

June 27, 2018 - late afternoon

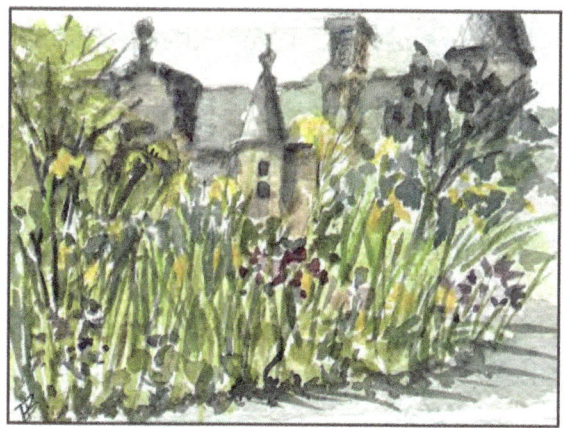

I sketched a little today — it felt good to slow down to the speed of simply looking at one thing for a long time. Everywhere I turn I want to take a photo; I rarely feel this way when I travel. It's odd, and I love it. The visual resting spots are even better.

June 28, 2018 - Thursday, trip to the coast

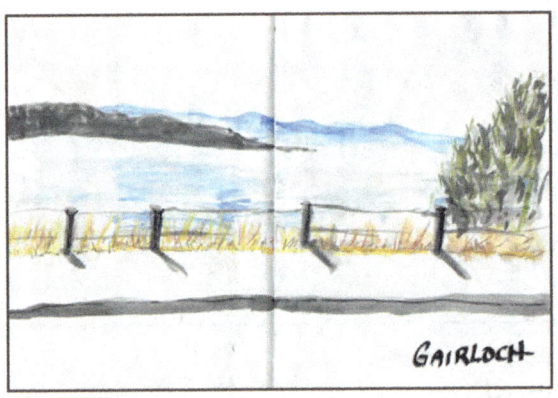

On the trip to the west coast of Scotland, I saw a sign that said, "Plot for Sale." I immediately thought J. K. Rowling might be interested…

I also learned that rowan trees give protection from faeries. Good to know.

June 29, 2018 - Friday, ten days in and we're almost finished

Once again, Road Scholar gets five stars for attention to detail! Aigas Field Centre gets much of the credit as well.

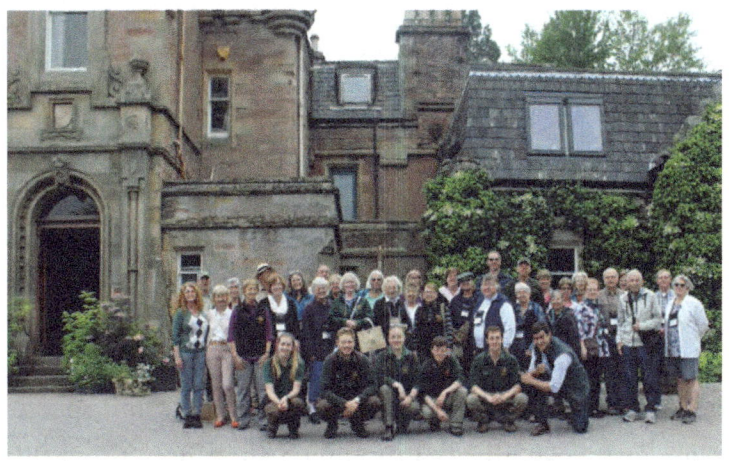

This is a photo of the entire crowd at the end of our trip- what a lovely group of Brits, Scots, and Americans. In the front row are our wonderful Rangers—environmental science students and educators. I'm so inspired. (That's me with the green cap, toward the center.)

June 30, 2018 - Saturday, last morning at Aigas

How odd, wonderful, that when it's almost time to go home, I suddenly feel ready to call it done. Odd because no matter how long or short the trip is, about 18 hours before it ends, I am pleasantly eager to get home.

I'm writing this sitting in the common room, all packed and ready. The woodstove door was just opened for a moment, and the faint aroma of wood smoke is comforting. Today is our second day in a row of classic cloudy Scottish weather—the only other overcast day was a week ago, the day after we all arrived at Aigas. Authentic weather bookends.

Listening to bagpipes playing "Highland Cathedral"

just now brought me to tears—not all bagpipe tunes do that. Maybe it's because we're leaving.

This trip was wonderful, far better than I expected, worth every penny. When we weren't in the baronial hall enjoying delicious meals, we were dashing off to explore outdoors. We eagerly climbed into the three coaches, listening to the brilliant young Rangers as they told us about ancient geological events, relevant details of Highland human history, and current efforts being made to restore ecological balance to lands and species that have been affected by the reckless presence of humans. Inspirational.

I also had an interesting epiphany: when you introduce yourself to total strangers, you're sometimes surprised at what you hear yourself saying.

July 3 - 2018- home in NH

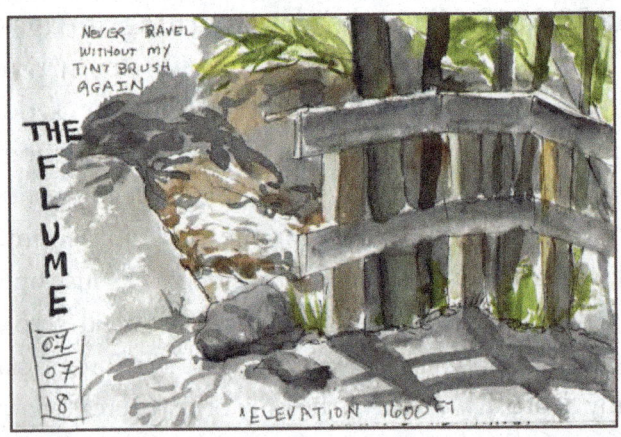

Back from Scotland, almost speechless for a couple weeks, hard to understand what is going on inside me.

First and clearest, I experienced a media-detox that grew each day we were in the Highlands. When I returned to my downtown home in New Hampshire, I had an aversion, rather than an addiction, to radio, TV, and the internet. At Aigas Field Centre, we had limited access to the internet, but only in the Common Room in the main house, and only at certain times of day. There was a total absence of radio and television, and in its place, we had the company of strangers who were becoming friends. The food was organic and so was the agenda; each day grew naturally out of the days that preceded.

I was the only one with a sketchbook, and only one other person, a birder, carried a small notebook where he jotted down sightings and notes from the field. Everyone else "took notes" by using their cameras.

I thoroughly enjoyed those three days in Glasgow before the rest of the group arrived, but it's not what I think of when I recall "my trip to Scotland." Instead, I recall the coach pausing in Glencoe, a beautiful valley-rift between two ridges, not unlike our own Franconia Notch, but on a much grander scale. The towering hills on either side of the road through the glen were impressive, and when I saw a group of specks on the hillside and realized it was a group of hikers, I had a much better sense of scale. Also, as it turns out, it was one of the few days with "Scottish" weather: clouds and fog giving way to sunlight, then dashing back to threatening rain yet again.

In Tomich, I asked one of the Rangers to take a picture of me while using my handmade "Look-at-That Art Pouch." He said, "Well, I could do that, but Pete is much better with a camera." Understatement! I found out later that Pete Short, one of the Rangers, had worked for the BBC as a cameraman and has his own professional photography business.

Pete and I talked a few times after that. I didn't want to monopolize his time or distract him from his work, but I felt a closeness to him. Pete and I don't need our cameras or sketchbooks in hand to be capturing images, designing compositions, subconsciously saying, "Look at that!" day and night, merely because we're awake and have our eyes open. It's a shift, a mental click, that's available to anyone. You can't force it, you can't even teach it, but once someone's seen it, there's no going back.

You find yourself with a constant ponder of "What would Ansel Adams see?" I don't really care what another artist would draw or paint. I care what they would *see*. The re-creation on paper, canvas, or film is secondary to the thrill of actually seeing with fresh eyes.

So, sketchbook in hand, I took notes on what I was seeing, not hoping to draw frameable art, or even create pretty pictures, but instead, with each pen-stroke, I was saying to every vista and to God, "Thank you!" Each mark on the paper has a subtext of, "I see you, you tree; I see you, you clump of heather; I see you, you stony crag, I love you, you fence post."

Sketching is just pointing, with your pen aimed down rather than out. "Look at that, and that, and that." I never realized that before.

July 7, 2018 - four days later, at The Flume Gorge, Lincoln NH

Well worth the climb and so happy to have this time alone here on the bench.

Tourists are a funny lot. There are young kids racing everywhere, not really giving a hoot about the scenery. Then there are the athletic adults, who admire the views, but only as they move along at a steady clip.

Finally, there are the slightly older slow walkers, who don't even qualify for the title of "hikers." They meander, pause, stretch, and take deep breaths now and then.

This sketch took a little while because there was so much to see, so much to distill. I was aware of the general hubbub around me, and after a while, I sensed a presence and looked up.

An elderly Japanese man was standing some distance away, carefully watching me work. Our eyes met. He smiled and bowed slightly a few times, the international sign for, "Ah, yes, continue, thank you, yes!"

I placed my hand on my heart and smiled back at him, deep breath. He was taking the time to enjoy the natural beauty, and to watch me play. I was fortunate to be able to travel to Japan thirteen years ago on business, and although it's silly to generalize, it seems appropriate to me that of all the people at the Flume with me today, it would be an elderly Japanese man who would take time to be fully present.

All those memories are packed into this little sketch, and no one would even know if I didn't enjoy writing and storytelling almost as much as I love sketching.

August 26, 2018 - test-driving ideas for future class handouts

I have so much I want to teach them, show them, and I know within minutes their eyes and hearts and minds will glaze over if I'm not careful. I feel like an overly eager teenager going on a date. I am ridiculous.

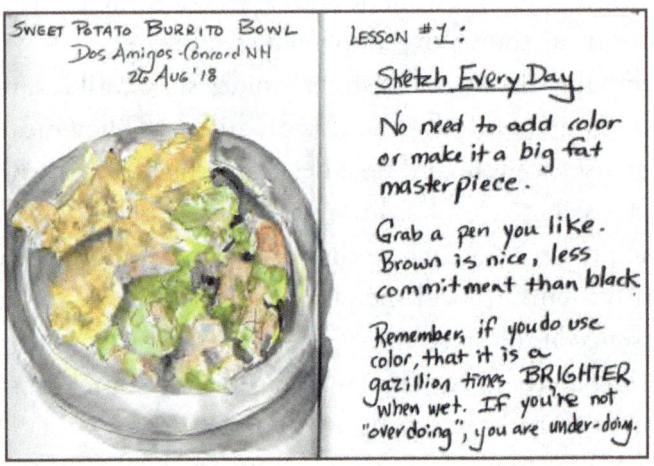

Lesson #1: Sketch Every Day

No need to add color or make it a big fat masterpiece. Grab a pen you like. Brown is nice, less commitment than black. Remember, if you add watercolor, the paint's a million times brighter when wet. If you're not "over-doing," you're actually "under-doing."

September 19, 2018 - journal notes

I know increasingly that the stories I tell myself about my life (sometimes around struggles, pity-seeking stories) are no different than ordering at the deli counter. *We get what we order.*

I experience as "real" anything I believe is memorable. I may not choose all my circumstances, but I do choose what memories to have framed and mounted on the walls of my mind's living room. There's a lot of power in that insight.

September 27, 2018 - 1pm

Comfy, sitting in the sun here at the Purple Pit Café in Bristol.

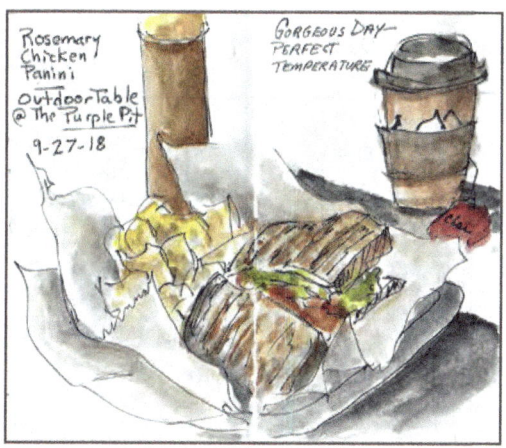

Delicious sandwich, chicken rosemary salad on grilled rye bread. Sitting outside, I'm amazed Bristol is a destination spot now. Perfect weather. So much fun juggling eating and sketching… that's why we order beautiful, room-temperature food, right?

November 21, 2018 - Wednesday noon

Just left retinal specialist emergency visit; tomorrow is Thanksgiving, so four-day weekend ahead means no access to help if needed. The eye doctor says that with my symptoms I'm sitting on a powder keg, not his words exactly, but that's my translation from "doctor-ese." Something bad is likely brewing, but since it's not present yet, there's nothing to do but "wait and see." That expression feels cruelly ironic at the moment. I cried in the parking lot, then put out the word on Facebook that I need to develop a team for the next emergency. I'm so tired of this, so many years of this.

November 22, 2018

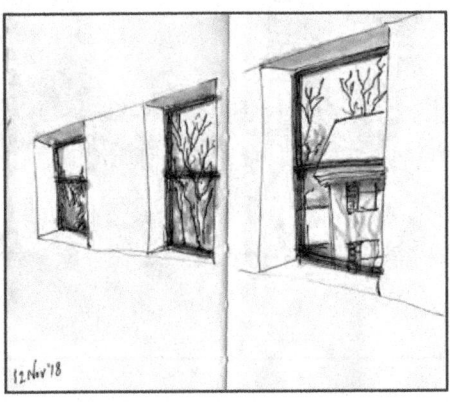

Even when I feel like a ticking bomb, it soothes me to simply hold a pen in my hand and a tiny sketchbook on my lap. I've no idea what's outside the windows, so I made it up.

Artistic license never expires.

December 17, 2018 - afternoon sketchbook notes

I sway between fear and anger and exhausted acceptance.

Today it ended with a therapeutic serving of ice cream and hot tea at 4pm, including a sketch of both, followed by yet another film about the life of Van Gogh. So many films about him have been produced in the past few years. *"At Eternity's Gate"* had 82% approval on Rotten Tomatoes. *"Loving Vincent"* was 85%. Excellent films.

I wonder sometimes, am I studying art, or suicide…

December 19, 2018 - Wednesday

Driving home from Warner after a wonderful five hours with Dana B. I noticed a little distortion in my vision on the way home, like the wobbly lines seen through antique glass windows. It may be another hemorrhage.

Maybe I'm just tired and scrutinizing things too much. Hard to tell old distortions from additional new ones. I need to write and paint and get things in order. This still feels like a very unstable time in my eyesight saga.

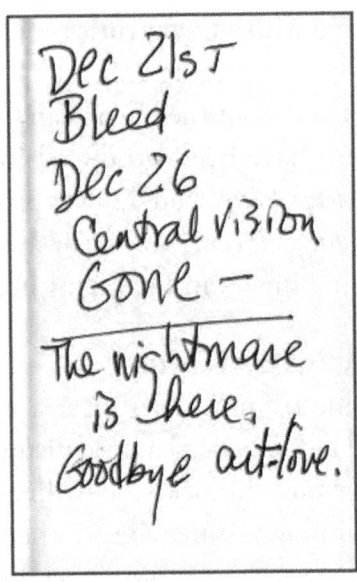

Funny, it doesn't show in my handwriting here, because I have such great muscle memory that I can write myself a note in the dark in the middle of the night with the light off, and it's perfectly legible. It doesn't show in my artwork either because although my design intentions and the actual results are miles apart, there's no visible evidence trail left between the two. Who would ever know except me?

But from my side of the eyeballs, everything is "FUBAR" as David used to say: "f'ed up beyond all recognition." I miss him so much. I want to call him and just hear him say, "Bobb, this sucks." That's all. My vision is like I'm drunk or tripping, every minute of the day. Nauseating situation, figuratively as well as literally sometimes.

I'm full of rage again, angry when I can't find what

I'm looking for, and then discover it's sitting on the table, right in front of me, in one of my new blind-spots. Damn it.

December 26, 2018 - Wednesday

A whole new experience of "blind contour drawing," not funny. There are new blind spots in the middle of my right eyesight, all within the last two hours — now 12:55am.

I'll "see" the retinal doctor at 3:30pm, in fourteen hours…

My eyesight was SO MUCH BETTER Sunday when I called for help.

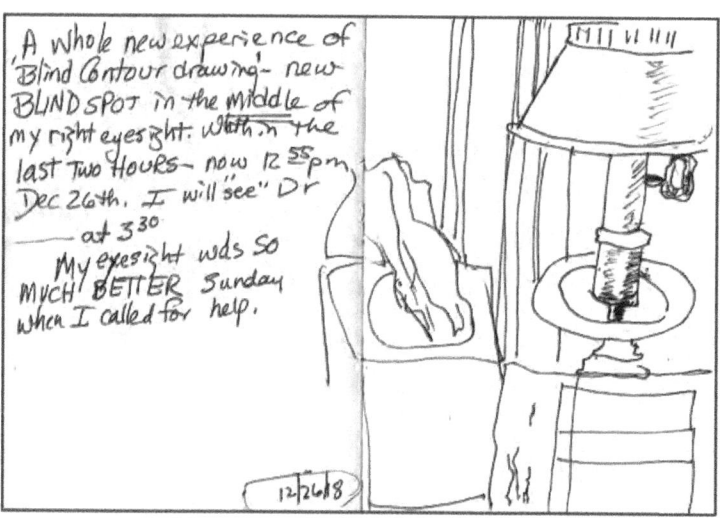

This is the second hemorrhage this year that's happened on a long holiday weekend: first on Thanksgiving, and now this. Waiting to see an MD is torture, knowing that the bleeding is simply continuing. Very depressed;

this hemorrhage started on December 19 and they won't be able to treat it until the 26th.

December 31, 2018 - New Year's Eve ponder

It's official: it's too late now for a full recovery. Time to give up my driver's license for good.

I'd give anything to have the eyesight I used to complain about.

Someday I may say the same thing about *today's* remaining vision.

Perhaps that's the lesson of a lifetime.

Be careful what you take for granted.

Chapter 7: 2019

Endings and Beginnings

January 2, 2019

Those sixty-three days of not driving in the summer of 2017 are a far cry from handing over my car keys today for the rest of my life. Sold my beloved gold Subaru Forester to a friend who needs it. No car of my own ever again, no rentals, nothing. Done driving. It's mind-boggling.

And of course, it's not just the "no driving" situation, it's the hard work of seeing life through a single permanently filthy lens, if I'm lucky. Secretly and silently, part of me is planning my exit from this world if the sight in my right eye vanishes now, twenty-seven years after the sight in the left one disappeared. This is the lowest point of my life. It feels like the final cymbal crash of a 45-year-long, 13-eye-surgery glaucoma drum roll, the grand finale. I'm too tired for words. Too tired for hope of any kind.

January 15, 2019 - late evening, two weeks later

With this newly reduced eyesight, I get overstimulated easily when I'm around people, especially if there's a lot of activity. Each hemorrhage caused massive distortion and new blind spots. With each injected treatment, the intraocular blood pool begins to recede. As a result, the retina ripples distorting my sight become less pronounced, but it takes time. It never goes completely back to "before-hemorrhage" visual acuity. That's why interpreting what I'm looking at has become a full-time job.

If I misinterpret something when I'm seated, it's merely annoying, but if I'm trying to walk around obstacles, it can be a disaster. My whole life has slowed down by necessity. My brain is working overtime to compensate.

January 18, 2019 - help is here

Regina from the NH Association for the Blind was here at the apartment today. It's so reassuring to have that organization in my back pocket; most of the equipment they provide is for people with more advanced blindness than I have right now. Regina's wise reassurances were invaluable; I don't want pity, not at all. I just need to know there will be kind, knowledgeable people there when I do need further help.

The organization also hosts a monthly peer support group where men and women of all ages and all stages of vision loss get together to check in, share joys and struggles, and encourage one another. For now, I have a bit more remaining sight than many of the peer members, and I sometimes feel self-conscious about that. Nevertheless, they welcomed me with open arms, saying, "We have each been where you are now, and it's not easy at any point in this journey."

January 27, 2019

I was at Dos Amigos having lunch a couple days ago, looking at the artwork on the walls. This is now the only place in town that shows local artists' work, and I asked the manager how far out they're booked. "Not that far," was her reply. "The next opening is March."

"Five weeks from now?" I said, surprised.

"Oh no," she smiled. "March 2020."

I grinned, pleased that there's such an active community of proficient artists here in Concord.

Much to my surprise, I went back to see her today with a printout of my last portfolio and signed up to have a show of my own framed work 13 months from now. No more line-and-wash sketches like I've been doing for the past several years. I can't see well enough to do that. My challenge now will be to go way back to the style I was pursuing in 1986 when my watercolor life began. It's a looser, more painterly approach to watercolor, in the style of Ron Ranson, my first watercolor hero. He was British and wrote wonderful instructional books, as well as creating videos that have inspired beginner watercolorists for decades.

I may be taking on far too much, but I'm going to give it a try. I desperately need a North Star to draw me forward in my life. I still want to see, and paint, what I can, while I can.

February 4, 2019 - sketchbook notes

My Montem trekking poles are my new "car." I walked back from the eye doctor appointment (which included another injection) and although I couldn't see the irregularities in the sidewalk, I felt much safer, using these poles for balance.

I'm more in touch with the tempo of life too, walking instead of driving around in a 4,000-pound metal box. This is my new world, not all bad.

February 20, 2019 - waiting for the bus

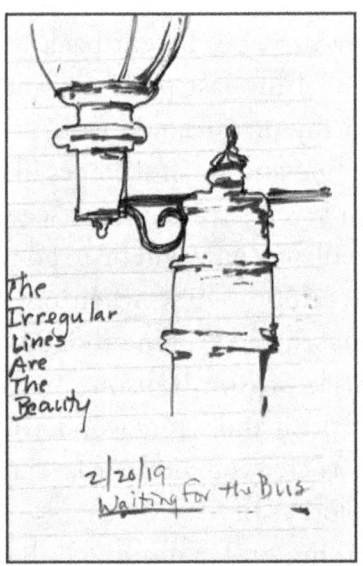

The irregular lines are the beauty.

March 3, 2019 - Kimball Jenkins, my first "Look at That Open House"

I'm working from a photo, one of many interesting images I brought to inspire and share with my guests today. Eleven people showed up, wonderful!

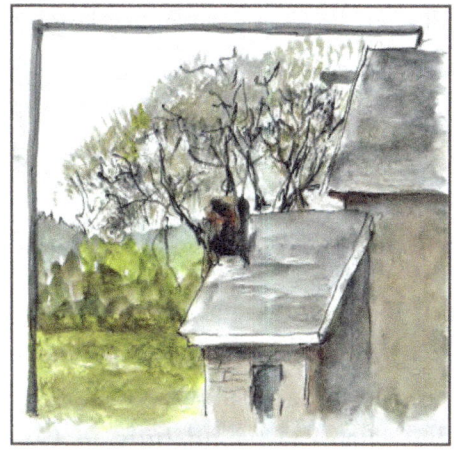

Many of them were personal friends; I take that as a compliment because some were budding artists, but others were just there to be supportive of what I'm trying to do. It was an open house, not a paid class, so I felt so much less pressure to see and understand everything going on around me. Great fun planting seeds of success together!

March 16, 2019 - Saturday after class

My first time, post-hemorrhage, trying to teach a full class at Kimball Jenkins, with even poorer eyesight than I had before and no car to help carry all my teaching supplies. I'm not sure this is going to work out. It's much harder now to see the facial expressions of the people at the other end of the table. If they hold up their sketchbook to show me where they're struggling, or what they're proud of, I have to stand up, walk over to them, take off my glasses and hold their book fairly close to my face. Everyone's very kind, of course, but it doesn't feel graceful or inspiring to me at all. This is not where I want their focus. Learning to sketch is about joy, not me and my stupid situation. Ugh.

March 20, 2019 - journal note

What a difference a day makes! I've felt frustrated and grumpy for weeks now. I can create all sorts of busywork, stumbling along, writing, painting, reading, whatever, but in the end, I have this voice inside saying, "Who cares?"

Then yesterday I had a delightfully long, unexpected video chat with my friend Judy in England. As a result, my wildest dream may turn into an actual plan. Even though I thought traveling would now be way beyond my comfort zone, I might be landing yet again in England in just seven weeks! It'll be my fifth visit to Great Britain, how lucky am I?

I need to rush to get my passport renewed, so I'm heading out to get that photo done shortly. It feels bizarre, impulsive, but if Judy's ready for a visitor (not a houseguest, of course!), then I think we're on our way.

March 21, 2019 - the deed is done!

I just bought my plane tickets online. I'm stunned that I'm doing this, but Judy seems excited. She might well be saying, *"Crikey, an American underfoot for over a week? I must be mad!"* I'll make sure I find ways to give her space, to explore places on my own.

April 4, 2019 - afternoon

I took the 11:44am bus to see the optometrist to find

out if I'm ready again for new eyeglass lenses. I've lost count; is this the third new refraction in less than two years? I have so little wiggle room in functional vision, I can barely see the big "E" at the top of the eye chart, and the cataract is changing fast. If new lenses can get me down two or three lines on the eye chart, it will change my daily life tremendously. And of course, why go on a trip overseas with dreadful eyesight if you can do anything to ease the difficulty? I'll reuse a pair of old frames, of course, to lessen the cost, but it's still outrageously expensive. The new eyeglass lenses cost about as much as the plane ticket.

I know I'm spending money that I should be saving for a rainy day, but in the last couple of years, it feels like it's been pouring, so what the heck? "I want to see what I can see, while I can see"—that's my mantra. I'm using that to justify this next trip.

April 7, 2019

I've lost my weekly Wednesday morning coffee companion—Kerry B. died two days ago. Casual friendships are so delightful, so easy to take for granted because taking them for granted is part of their allure: the fact that I could count on it without question.

Kerry became such a dear friend, despite us being on polar-opposite sides of the American political divide. That was one of the most precious things about it: we held our friendship in higher esteem than the things that usually tear people apart. We acknowledged there's a great deal we don't have in common, but that we want to explore and cherish the values we do share. I'm quite proud of that. I suspect I'll miss him more than I realize quite yet. Yet another reminder that none of us has any time to waste.

On with the day. I'm good at starting things, less experienced at finishing them, and I've been told that completion is where the deepest satisfaction lies.

I've been thinking of Mom a lot lately, and I choke up just writing this. If it weren't for her love and her inspired frugality, I wouldn't have the luxury to live as I do today, or to travel at all. I'm careful with day-to-day expenses because I'd rather be able to travel than have pretty clothes and a fancy home. My splurges nowadays are the rare fancy coffee at a cafe and a new bottle of fountain pen ink—both feel delightfully sinful.

May 6, 2019 - Monday, to Logan Airport in Boston

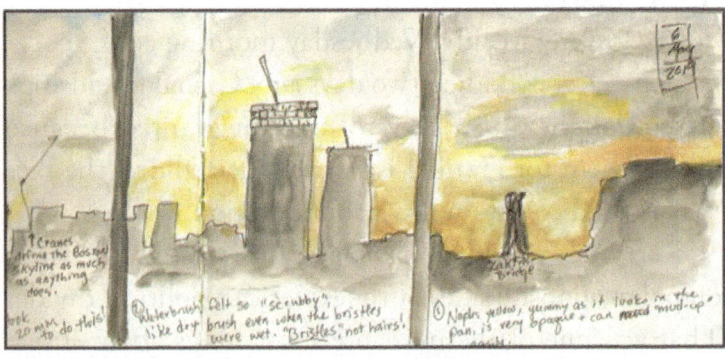

7:40pm- Gate E12 is at the very end of a series of long corridors in this airport, as usual. Are any of those gates I passed along the way ever used? Perhaps they're for much smaller planes.

This is Travel Day Zero, in a new sketchbook, with a new view. I started on the right side of this two-page image, because that's where the sunset was changing fast. The Zakim Bridge looks so odd from this angle. I used a bit of Naples yellow in the sky, yummy color, but it can "mud-up" easily when mixed with other colors. Middle window panel: the water brush felt so "scrubby," like drybrush even when the bristles were wet. Yes, "bristles," not hairs! The ubiquitous construction cranes define the skyline in Boston.

May 7, 2019 - 3am body time, 35 minutes left in the flight

I've slept about an hour, thank goodness. The seat back in front of me is about four inches from my nose at the moment, so it's not conducive to in-flight sketching. The flight attendant is distributing customs declaration forms, and I feel like an old hand at this, even though I never traveled alone until a few years ago, when I turned sixty years old.

Later… Judy met me at Heathrow in London, so amazing to finally meet her in person after being great pals online for two full years. She surprised me with a swing through RHS Wisley on the way home to Fleet. Wow! I was here at these gardens a couple years ago on a whirlwind Road Scholar trip. At the time, it was pouring rain, so today's sunshine was delightful.

May 8, 2019 - Day Two is off to an odd start

When I bought my plane ticket back in March, I also made reservations for the entire time at a hotel near Fleet. I ignored Judy's skeptical frown when she learned I'd made reservations there.

The room assigned to me (for a nine-day, overseas traveler's visit) was barely big enough to be a broom closet: no table, no chair, no bureau, no closet, only a bed and two hooks on the wall. There was a bathroom, but no room to close the bathroom door once you were in there. Their website had apparently kept this room a secret!

I was so exhausted and jet-lagged when we arrived yesterday that all I wanted was to lie down. But after one night, I knew I had to find other accommodations. Bit of a panic because every local place was booked out for weeks. Judy scrambled and worked her magic! A nearby bed-and-breakfast had a last-minute cancellation that fit my schedule perfectly. I repacked, and we moved all my things over to the B&B, took a deep breath, and started again.

Judy also had a grand surprise waiting for me right away on our first full day together: a late afternoon Cream Tea Cruise on the Basingstoke Canal, glorious!

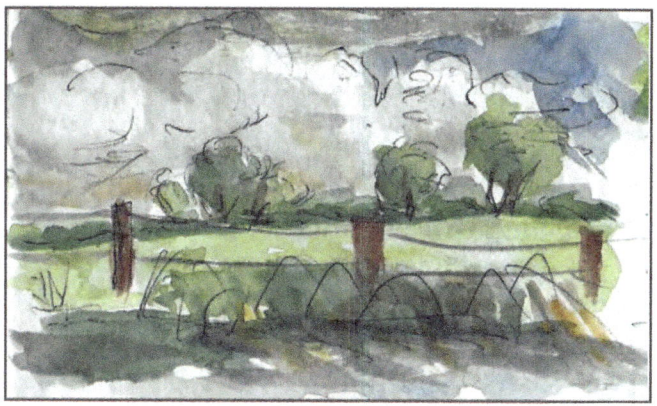

I did this sketch using ink first, then added splashes of color. The narrowboat kept moving along, of course, so the clouds, trees, field, and river grasses are from several different sections of the canal.

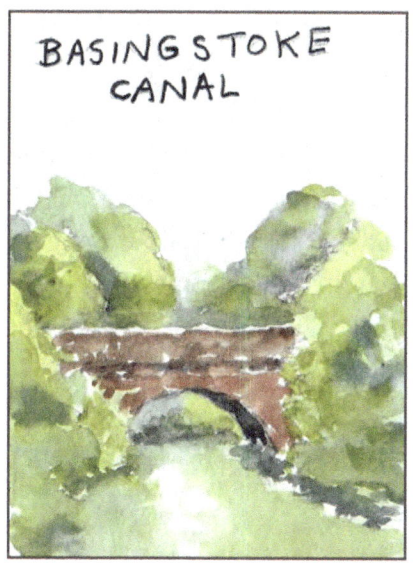

I did this second sketch tonight, back at the B&B,

from a photo I took today. Sketches done on-site always look much "sketchier" than this! I'm really pleased with the brushwork, a lot of restraint.

Day 3 - traveling with the W.I. ladies on a bus tour to Leonardslee Gardens

Judy had to work today, so I signed up for a bus trip to a garden spot in Horsham, about an hour southeast of here. When I arrived at the bus stop in Fleet, I realized most of the women getting on the coach knew one another: they were members of the Fleet chapter of the Women's Institute. I stood toward the end of the line, and got the last seat, wedged into the back row with two other women who were pleasant enough, but reserved. I'm sure even my two-syllable word, "sorry," gave away my American accent.

A few miles down the road, one of my seat mates started a polite conversation with me, and by the time we arrived at the Gardens an hour later, the nearby ladies said they were willing to help me with just about anything. They said I could follow along with them, but I explained I would be sketching and didn't want to hold anyone up.

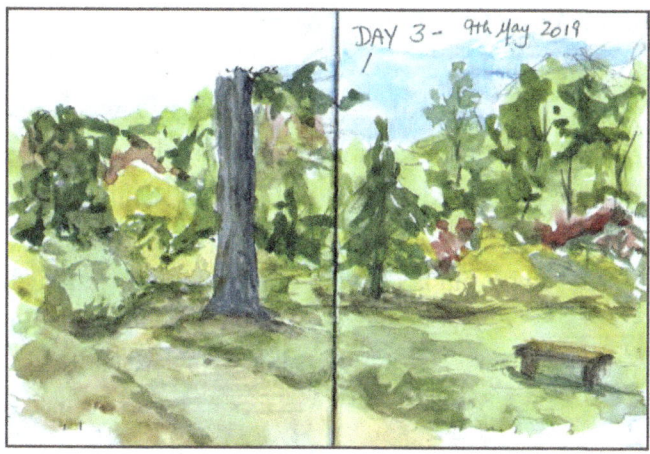

I did several sketches, mostly not great, but the time spent there was pure pleasure. The rhododendrons and azaleas were spectacular. I must have arrived at the height of the season. I took so many pictures, especially as the weather changed from clear and dry to black scuttling thunderheads. In late afternoon there was a stunning cloudburst, but luckily by then I was cozied up in the café with a scone, raspberry jam, and a little pot of Earl Grey tea.

The bus ride home included "the passing of the sketchbook" throughout the coach. The ladies were so kind and appreciative, but not stunned to see a well-used sketchbook, unlike people back home. We Americans have amputated so much natural creativity from our experiences of daily life. For many American women, their creativity often begins and ends with cooking, gardening, and raising families. That's grand too, of course, but I'm so glad I can always carry a "toybox" that fits in my purse: sketchbook, pen, palette, and brush.

Day 5 - May 11, 2019

I came outside early today, hoping to have time to sketch the lovely entrance garden here at Dawyck Beech Guest House before Judy meets me for the day's adventure. This place and the hosts here made all the difference in my vacation; it was an absolute miracle that a room was available for five of the seven days remaining.

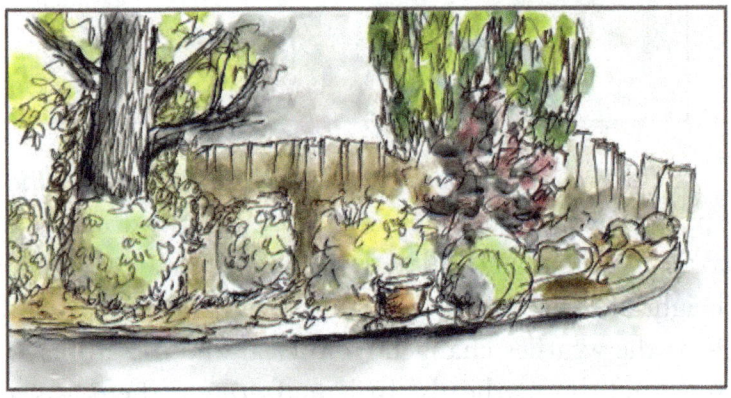

This morning, Judy and I were off to Hook (I love the names of towns here!), about eight miles by car. West Green House Garden has been owned by the National Trust since 1971, and Alistair McAlpine restored the gardens and added monuments, follies, and all sorts of interesting outdoor spaces to please visitors. There's one 50-foot column with a Latin inscription that reads: "This monument was built with a great deal of money which otherwise someday would have been given into the hands of the public revenue." Love it.

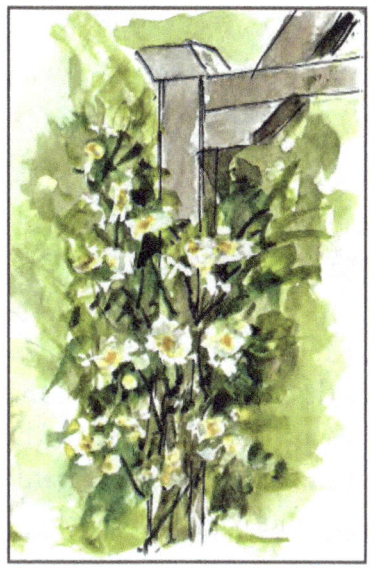

Learning the history of the place added so much to the experience of being here. A faction of the Irish Republican Army apparently bombed the house in 1990. Three years later, Marylyn Abbott (a marketing and tourism professional from Australia) led the restoration.

She states, "I have been looking for a ruined garden and thought the house was beautiful and so it catered to all my needs." Her love of opera and experience with the Sydney Opera House are reflected in the regular opera performances offered there.

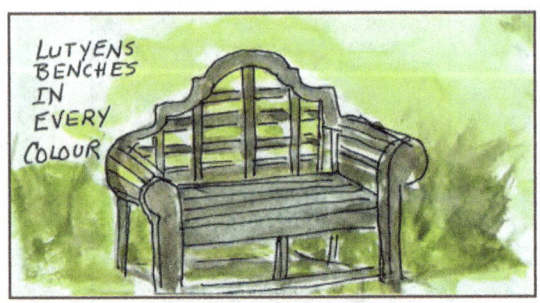

A beautiful day, wandering with Judy along the winding paths, through "rooms" and manicured water gardens. Lutyens' benches, inspired by the British architect, Sir Edwin Lutyens, dotted the gardens, and made restful pondering and sketching much easier.

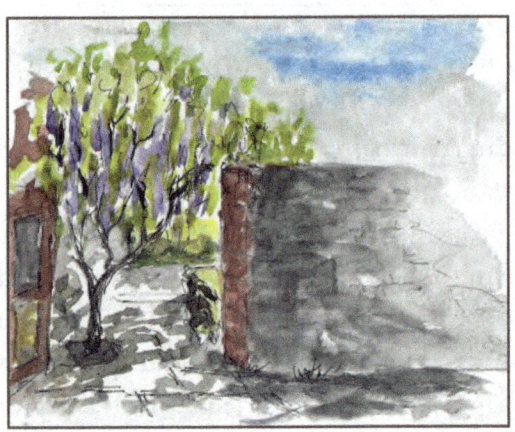

The surprise wisteria beyond the brick wall took my breath away.

May 12, 2019 - Day 6- We're off to the coast!

What a treat to be traveling to where Judy grew up on the southern coast of England. The seaside café in

Goring, where we're seated right now, is at the end of long rows of colorful beach huts. I've ordered lunch, but the view of the sea is so powerful, so many colors in the water itself, that I'm far more interested in sketching than eating. Pure heaven. I want to sprinkle the salt air, gentle breeze, and smell of beach food right into this watercolor paper.

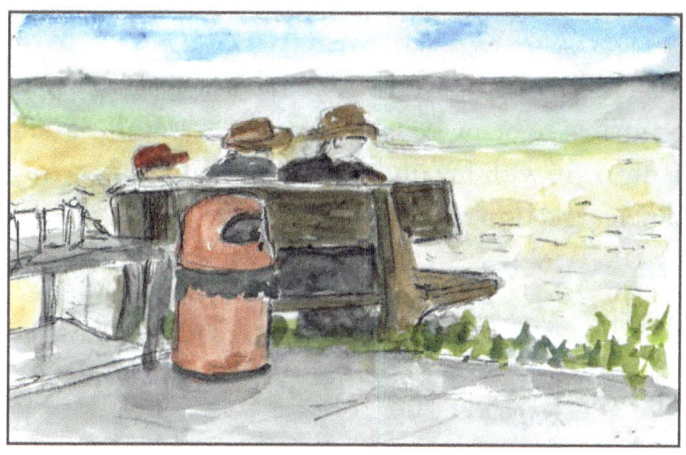

The three people sitting on the bench in front of me look quite settled in, but you never know! Time to scratch in some quick pen work before they move away. Their hats make me smile. Their posture betrays their ages, no spring chickens here! These folks earned those seats on the bench over many years. I could have left out the trash barrel, but it's so colorful, and adds a bit of truth to the scene.

May 13, 2019 - Monday, Day 7 - Odiham

Forty-one miles southwest of London, an entire

world away. This town of about 4,400 souls is listed in the 1086 Doomsday Book, so it's been here a while. Odiham Castle was built in 1207-1214, halfway between Windsor and Winchester. The amount of history that British kids must learn makes national history lessons in America feel paltry. (Of course, descendants of European settlers wrote my textbooks, intentionally excluding the indigenous people who were here long before 1776.)

Here on Day 7, Judy is at work again, and I feel acclimated to being here in England, to walking around on my own, with my undisguisable American accent. So many gorgeous days in a row.

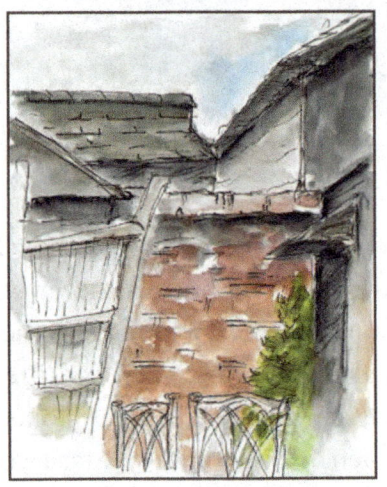

10:40am - As I was walking along the pavement ("sidewalk" for you Yanks), I looked in and spotted the Creperie's garden patio with tables and a wonderful skyline of angular roofs. Not at all hungry, but to help pay the table rent (as we sketchers must do to show how grateful we are), I ordered an apricot crepe and pot of English Breakfast tea. Here I sit, in the shade, in a French café in the middle of England. My heart can't take much more delight than this.

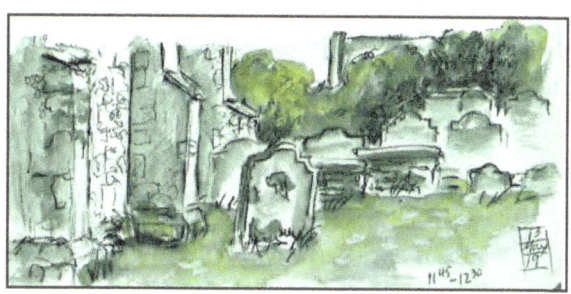

Later, same day... sitting by the 11th century All Saint's Church here in Odiham. There's been a church on this site from as far back as 1086. According to the bronze plaque, the base of the tower is the oldest part. The buttresses and windows are all from different times, different styles.

There are so many benches to choose from here in the churchyard. This very moment is so alive; birds are singing like mad, and there are very few human sounds, despite its being in the middle of a town. A distant lawnmower was purring along until it suddenly jammed and stopped—no doubt hit a rock from the sound of it. It's pleasantly windy and chilly at the moment, my windbreaker jacket perfect comfort.

I love sitting here, quietly sketching, also recording a couple of short videos, all to capture this very moment. Behold the lilies of the field, the daisies of the churchyard. I catch myself thinking, over and over again, "I'm in England, I'm in England." And when I am here, I feel I'm home.

May 15, 2019 - heading back to America, 2pm over the Atlantic

Ground speed: 563 mph. Altitude: 39,327 feet. Flight time remaining: 4 hours, 15 minutes.

Just finished watching *"Stan and Ollie,"* the in-flight movie, how perfect. I was stunned when I saw a scene in the film that was shot in Worthing, on the very pier where Judy and I were standing three days ago. Next there were more film scenes in the cafe on the pier where Judy and I had our lunch!

Sadly, I'm not in England anymore, but I'm not yet in America either. I remember the reaction I had to being back in the States after the Scotland trip a year ago. I'm taking a deep breath because I know the transition will once again be jarring.

At the core, of course, it's not about America or Britain. Nothing beats having exciting plans, whether on a trip or at home. I find fallow time difficult; where's my faith, or even my simple recollection? Fallow is just a bit of a rest, the prelude to future adventures.

On this trip, with native Brit Judy, I felt my voice soften the longer I was there. I like how I was feeling, how I was behaving, at that easy tempo. I'm "really chuffed," proud that the entire trip was a rousing success.

When I'm finally home later today, I'll let the laundry, grocery-shopping, and scurrying around wait a while, and instead savor the aftermath and gifts of this trip. It'll be downright odd to see Judy on Zoom in a few days, and her cat Jessie! I am so blessed.

June 2, 2019 - second open house at Kimball Jenkins

No idea how long I'll offer these free sessions, but today was certainly fun. My architect friend Patrick stopped by, and it was a treat to see his approach, methodical and assured. Sketching and painting for the fun of it differs greatly from the precision required for professional architectural renderings. Fascinating, I love when everyone in the room becomes the teacher.

June 6, 2019 - a shift in painting focus

I recently signed up for an affordable art class online, to keep learning, growing. My first choice was Andy Walker and I'm so glad! His approach is simple, clear, priceless. No matter what your skill level is, he cheerfully encourages you to, "Give it a go!"

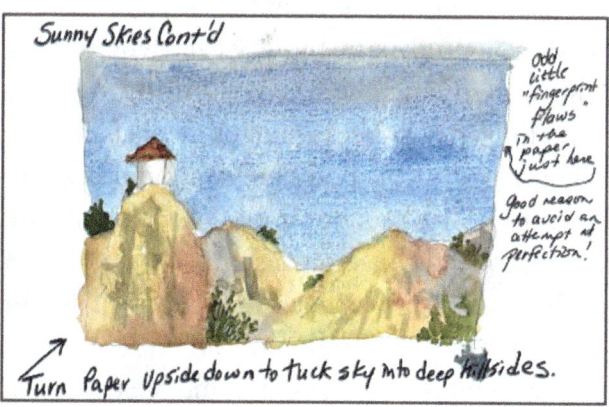

His classes are on Udemy, a website I've not used before, but it's user-friendly, and lifetime access is great. I signed up for "Paint Landscapes in Watercolor, Parts 1 & 2." So far, so good.

June 7, 2019 - Friday

Just got back from Red River Theatre where I saw the 2018 film, *All Is True*. I plan to go see it again on Sunday. It's about the private life of William Shakespeare, fictionalized of course, but it touched my heart, even beyond the superb all-star cast. I'm drawn to any tale that explores the dichotomy of a person's inner vs. outer life. It's so easy to think that what we see on the outside is the truth, possibly the whole truth. I doubt it is ever so.

June 26, 2019

Today I received my copy of the stunning book, *The Apocalypse Variations* by Marc Taro Holmes. This man, who has been an encouraging leader and instructor in the Urban Sketching movement of the last decade, has pushed past painting from rigorous on-site observation, to envisioning and painting a world where the glorious landscapes (which he has so skillfully portrayed for years) no longer exist because of climate change.

The images in this book are stark and dramatic, as are his words. He offers no simple answers, instead conveying a personal sense of despair, loss, and finally a small glimmer of hope that there may still be time to stop the insanity surrounding us all.

I look around my own country and see that it's on fire

and all I can offer to help put out the flame is a metaphorical teacup of water. It's not enough to just not add to the problem; I want to find a way to be part of the solution. But sad to say, other than voting and being a generally decent person, I've yet to find a civic duty niche for myself.

The Apocalypse Variations strikes me as a new way to vote. It serves as a warning. I wonder if I could help people fall in love with the world while we still have it. Something to ponder while sketching.

July 6, 2019 - A shift in my own artwork

I just ordered ten full sheets of 22x30 inch Saunders Waterford watercolor paper, enough to make forty decent-sized paintings for the show coming up in just seven months! My newest mentor (online, of course) is Lois Davidson, a modern English watercolorist whose teaching is so gentle, so generous. Some of her work reminds me of Ron Ranson's loose style. His misty, evocative work still enchants me.

I feel like a beginner these days, especially when I try juicy, direct watercolor, with no safety net of a preliminary under-drawing. I haven't done that for decades.

But here's the good news: the best way to cash in on watercolor's supposed "uncontrollability" is to just dive in! (Do other people give themselves pep-talks in their journals like I do??) I just need to accept that some perfectly good paper will have to hit the wastebasket before I'm finished. So what? Dash right in and, above all, enjoy. That's where the freshness and beauty reside.

August 9, 2019

Just finished writing the new description for my next series of classes at Kimball Jenkins. It's such a challenge to balance my desire to give people plenty of time to relax, while not having the class be so long that it is prohibitively expensive. I wish I could hand them a book that contains everything I want them to know, just the basics of art instruction, but with buckets of joy and motivation! That's what takes so long to convey, especially with so many adult women students who are bent on doing everything "right," as if there even is such a thing.

September 10, 2019 - sketchbook notes

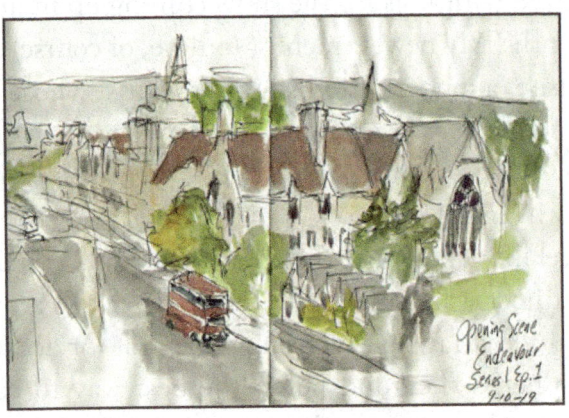

I spend a lot of time watching TV, especially late in the day when I don't have the energy for much else. If there's a scene in a film I particularly like, I can enjoy it even longer by pausing the screen and sketching it. This is how to travel overseas without leaving your living room.

September 13, 2019 - Friday

It's wonderful being back in my "junk sketchbook." I think of my Belgian friend, Debora, who loves painting on thin paper like this, precisely because it *does* buckle! The crinkly sound of the painted pages makes me smile, reminding me of her. That sound, as well as the wrinkly pages, become part of the beauty of the book.

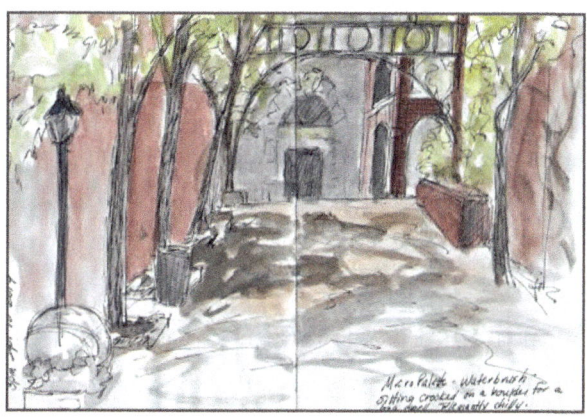

I'm finally pleased with this sketch today. It had to be rescued a couple times, but I've learned that if I'm dissatisfied, it's usually because the "pop" is still missing; that spot of contrast that draws the viewer in. Here it's the sunlight on the side of the clock tower at the top of the hill. I had to lift some of the shadow on the granite building to the left of the tower. Not fully successful, but better. I love learning.

September 17, 2019 - back in Bicentennial Square

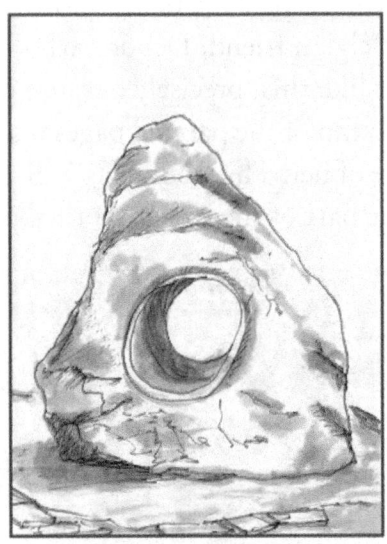

After a productive day doing dreary administrative work at my desk, I rewarded myself with a short walk outside. How fun to have a city park right outside my building, that I can pretend is the "east garden of my country estate."

The stone sculptures are fascinating to look at, and even more fun for little kids who climb on, around, and through them. Playing hide and seek with clever parents is the most fun of all.

October 7, 2019

I took part in "Inktober" for a while this year, a playful online month-long event created by Jake Park in 2009. The organizers assign a word to each day of October, and participants create a drawing based on that single word. The submissions tend to be ink-line only, thus the name, but there are no hard and fast rules.

These were fun to create since I don't work from my imagination often. Truth be told, after each word sparked an image in my brain, I went searching for a photo or object to help me draw the idea! Some of them took a lot of thinking. For the October 3rd word, "bait," I had no interest in drawing a worm, yuck, but when I thought of "a carrot vs. a stick," I realized a carrot can be a kind of bait. By the 6th word ("husky") I was just becoming silly.

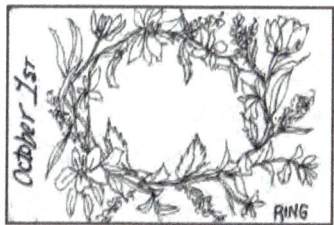

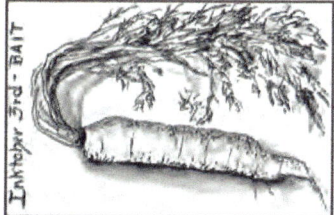

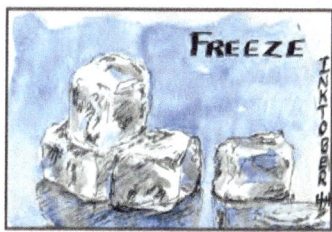

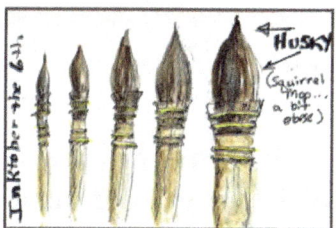

November 2, 2019 - in Boston

What a great day, my first time in person with the Urban Sketchers Boston group!

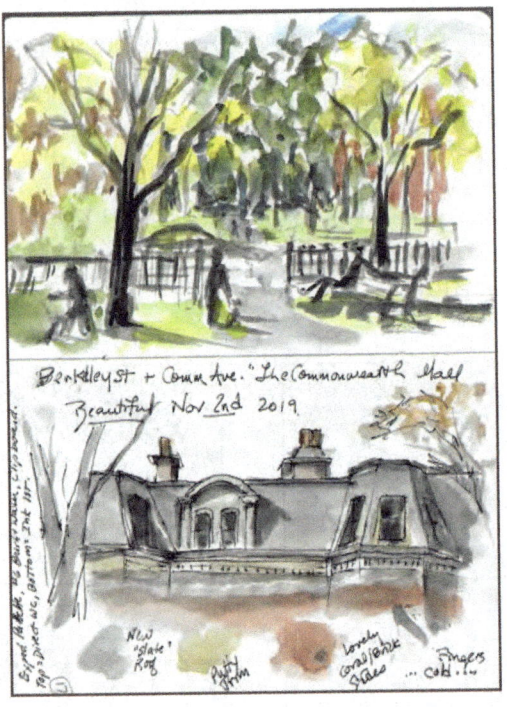

I met up with my niece Carra and her delightful friend Joanna, and we traveled together to the gathering spot for the day. Urban Sketchers Boston meets every weekend, year-round, and they announce the meet-up spot (usually outdoors, sometimes indoors) three or four days in advance. There were a dozen or so artists there, they were so welcoming.

November 21, 2019 - lunchtime

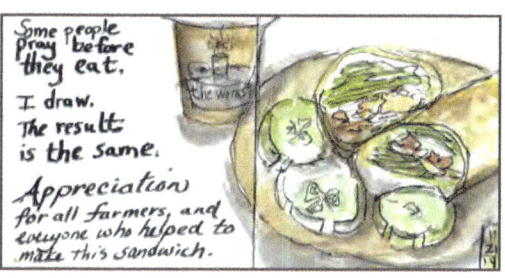

Some people pray before they eat. I draw. The result is similar: deep appreciation for all the forces, farmers, and other people who helped to make this sandwich.

December 26, 2019 - it only takes a moment

Well, that was easy. In one fell swoop, forgetting there was a cup of tea sitting in my blind spot, I just knocked it over, right into my laptop. Killed the motherboard instantly. No idea when I last backed up everything to the cloud or to an external hard drive. It took a while to get from "Oh, s**t" to "Oh well."

It's amazing, though, how quickly I triaged my way to pulling out a journal and carrying on writing, since the computer was no longer an option. I swear my blood pressure goes down, simply by having a pen in my hand. The cost of a new laptop will hurt. The consolation, though, is that I'm a non-techno girl at heart. I love sketchbooks and journals; have since I was fourteen years old. Thank goodness sketchbooks can survive a bit of rain, if not a whole fresh cup of English Breakfast tea.

Chapter 8: 2020

A Booklet? Possibly a Book?

January 3, 2020 - Friday

After a hard financial gulp, I picked up my new laptop today. Luckily, they could rescue the data on the hard drive, so there wasn't much damage except to my checkbook. Wonder if I'll ever feel safe again drinking liquids within six feet of it! Such an easy, expensive error.

January 14, 2020 - journal notes

I have just one more class to teach at Kimball Jenkins. It was a tough decision to make, and even harder to call the school to tell them a few days ago. I know it's time. A combination of things brought me to this decision:

External: Since I no longer drive a car, carrying all the teaching materials in a backpack and walking to the school is tough, especially in the winter. Taking a taxi just cuts into the little money I'm making. It's hard to see the students' facial expressions and their work when they're at the other end of the table, only eight feet away. Also, the director (who was my champion and was always great for a pep talk) is no longer there, so I feel a bit disconnected from the school itself.

Internal: I've been practicing my traditional watercolor skills again, to create framed paintings for the March 2020 show. Doing large format, frameable direct watercolor is so different from playing in a sketchbook, and I find it hard to switch back and forth quickly between the two. The show focus must come first now.

January 31, 2020

Keep Going AFTER You Give Up- Then You Have Nothing to Lose!

February 8, 2020 - Saturday, last class at Kimball Jenkins

What a lovely turnout for the last hurrah; I'm so pleased. Now the slate's clean, and I'm open to the next adventure.

Framing the new watercolors for the show has felt good this week, like a ritual blessing with many steps. Signing the painting is my signal to, "Stop fiddling; it's done!"

Next, tape it to the pre-cut mat board, wash the glass, mount the glass and matted art into the frame, secure the frame back together, then one last smiling glance before I add it to the pile of finished pieces. "So far, so good," yet again!

February 22, 2020

My first use of Daniel Smith's Caput Mortuum watercolor paint.

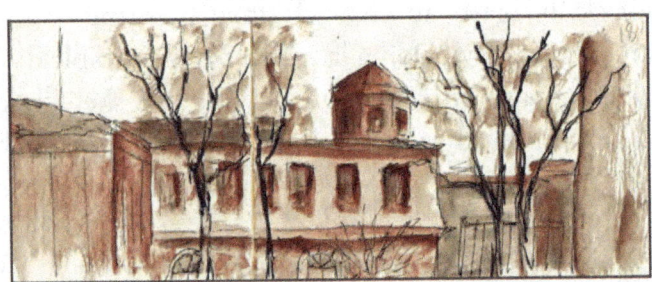

This mysterious color reminds me of the conte crayons we used in art school in the 1970s, that rich earth red I associate with the old masters. I still have my copy of 150 *Masterpieces of Drawing*, selected by Anthony Toney and published by Dover, © 1963. I probably bought it not long after that year. The book contains beautiful black-and-white images, and happily, the cover shows an earthy red Michelangelo study. The caption says he used red chalk in this drawing.

Conte crayons, invented in 1795, long after Michelangelo's death, are made of graphite and clay compressed together. They were created in response to a shortage of graphite during the Napoleonic Wars. Further research on caput mortuum paint led me down countless gory rabbit holes. Suffice it to say that yes, the name translates to "dead head," and the color is reminiscent of dried blood. I find it funny that "caput" means "head", but we often use the word "kaput" to mean hopelessly broken. Yes, there are days when my caput feels quite kaput!

February 25, 2020 - Tuesday late evening

The show is finally ready to hang on Sunday morning, phew. I've created my usual catalog and sales checklist because I want to have a record of where each one of these babies goes after they're sold. I wonder if other artists are as attached to their work as I am to mine. I'm going to paste thumbnails of a few of them here in my journal, so the art and the heart can stay together.

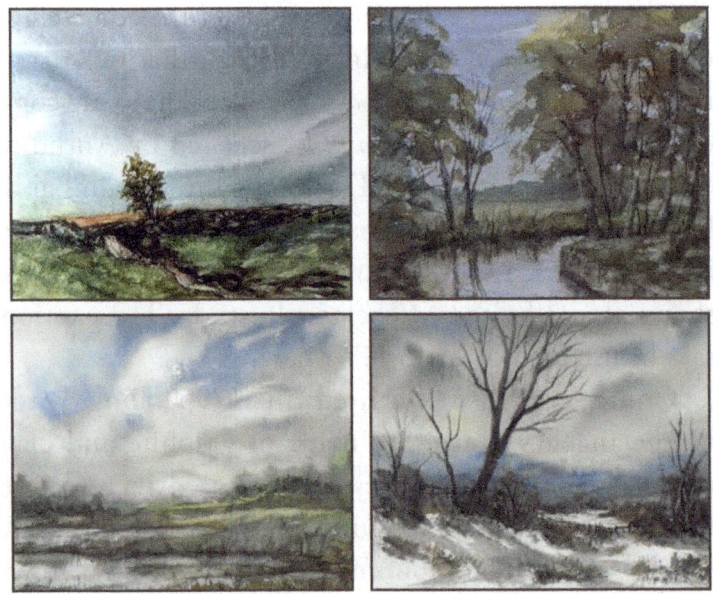

February 28, 2020 - Saturday evening

My March 2020 watercolor show's finally ready to hang tomorrow morning, and my heart is wandering off to future travel schemes.

It started when I posted a picture on Facebook's "Women of Road Scholar" page. It was of my Yorkshire painting of that single tree and the stormy sky (the one I pasted above here). It got a lot of "likes" and encouraging comments. It got me thinking, *"I bet there's a ready-made group of people right here who'd enjoy travel-sketching like I do."*

I've used a sketchbook on all my Road Scholar trips. Invariably, part way into the trip, a travel companion has asked if they could pass my sketchbook around the group at dinnertime. Several tour-mates even said, "I never thought to bring my sketchbook before. I'll be sure to pack it next time!"

Then it dawned on me: I could invent a brand-new kind of itinerary and send it to Road Scholar in Boston.

The idea was simple: A "Travelers-with-Sketchbooks Tour," with me as the artist-in-residence. I laid out the plan using their current English "Romance to Turbulence" itinerary as the template. That was a great trip, my very first with them back in 2012, and it's where I fell in love with the Lake District and Northumberland.

The only significant change to the original itinerary would be to add one more day at the beginning, at the beautiful Lindeth Howe Hotel in Bowness-on-Windermere, England.

On Day One, my plan will be to teach "First-Things-First Plein Air Sketching," which is a world apart from doing slow, methodical watercolors at your comfortable table at home with all the time in the world. It's almost like the difference between jotting down notes in shorthand and scribing illuminated calligraphy!

In the first morning's demonstrations, I'll set a timer for five, ten, and then fifteen minutes, to show how to manage sketching anything in a brief window of time. It's a critical skill to learn and practice if you plan to sketch outside when there may be storm clouds on the horizon, or if you'll be traveling with friends and family who want to move along!

Then each morning thereafter, when we arrive at each site, I would invite participants to pick a spot, watch the time, and relax into fun note-taking by sketching. Each evening before dinner, we'd have a show-and-tell time to share what we had learned, what surprises we'd encountered. By the end of the twelve days, they would have exciting skills it normally takes years to acquire, as well as, hopefully, a delightful new sketching habit.

I got so excited writing up the proposal, explaining how it would be nothing like the classroom-style painting experiences Road Scholar currently offers. Instead, it will be a brand-new, full-immersion dive into plein-air travel sketching.

I sent the proposal to Kelsey, my contact at Road Scholar, and now, less than a week later, I've received her enthusiastic response. She loved the proposal, and it's already in the hands of the VP of Programs. Fingers crossed!

Who says I don't want to teach anymore? Silly me!

March 1, 2020 – Sunday evening

Wow, it's late at night, and I want to capture how amazing today was.

It was a high-pressure sprint to get those twenty-seven paintings hung this morning before the restaurant opened, and there was no way on earth I could have pulled it off without the help of J. She has been such a great friend; I am so lucky. After we were all done, I raced home for a shower and a quick change of clothes before heading back for the opening reception at 1pm.

Immediately, ten people wanted to buy paintings. I thanked each person, then told them that the show was "pay now, pick up later" because I want the show to look complete for the entire month of March, like in a gallery art show. The red "sold" dots kept popping up, and by a few hours later, there were only a couple of paintings left available for sale.

Many people commented that these one-of-a-kind original works of art (each one matted, glassed, and framed) were underpriced. I price my work as low as possible, because my closest friends are not rolling in money, and I want these to be affordable. Most people I know don't even own an original piece of artwork; I want to change that.

March 8, 2020 - Sunday, a week later

First real rumblings of coronavirus fears are becoming real locally. I've been so hunkered down, getting those paintings finished and ready to hang, that I feel like I just arrived on the planet. This could be the beginning of a frightening new world.

March 14, 2020 - at White Mountain Gourmet Coffee Café

The panics are beginning, and it's hard to know what to make of it. I try to stay in the moment, recognizing this sketch at my favorite café may be the last one for a very long time.

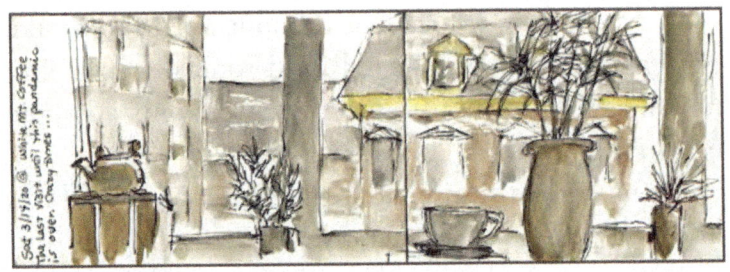

I'm already so grateful to all the medical professionals who won't have the luxury of isolating and working from home because they'll be busy saving our lives. Even taking a deep breath to calm down feels risky. These are uncharted waters for all of us.

March 17, 2020 - 8:30am

At Concord Eye Care, fingers crossed, hoping this ends up being a routine quarterly check-up. Early weeks of the COVID-19 pandemic; it's odd to be sitting in a public building, but luckily social-distancing is easy because only emergency appointments are being allowed. After all these years, I guess I'm considered a chronic eye emergency, which I'm grateful for right now. I left my phone at home by mistake, which makes me happy that this 3.5 by 5.5-inch Moleskine sketchbook never leaves my purse.

I'm so grateful the opening of my art show happened before the corona virus situation became urgent to us here, locally. The celebratory reception a mere seventeen days ago—the music, the noise, the intimate laughter—already seems like it was another world. The news now says to "prepare for 6 to 8 weeks of this lockdown." That may be far better than we can hope for. I look forward to the days of rational caution, rather than this full-blown panic. Borrowing trouble to steel ourselves against being surprised seems to be part of human nature. What is it we really fear?

I think we fear being surprised, more than we fear difficult situations.

Otherwise, why would we work so hard to anticipate every eventuality, even those in the distant future? I see so many forks in the road ahead of us in life, what good does it do to rehearse every possible outcome? My own life has taught me that no amount of planning prevents bad things from happening. If I insist on always making my life totally safe, I will miss all those beautiful "dandelion moments" right at my feet. This corona quarantine of the entire planet is humanity's time-out in the naughty chair. Overdue, I'd say.

First things first: I now feel responsible for the welfare of my paintings still on the wall at the restaurant, since I asked all the buyers at the grand opening two weeks ago to leave the artwork hanging on the wall for the balance of the month. Little did I know! Four days ago, on March 13th, I notified the local customers that they should pick up their paintings soon. I told my out-of-town patrons that I would get their paintings back to my apartment before the restaurant locks up for the foreseeable future. I hope to retrieve the remaining paintings at the restaurant as soon as I get back downtown this afternoon.

I just rubbed my itchy nose and instantly panicked!

Do we all feel like ticking time bombs now? Life is changing so fast, and yet I just heard a burst of laughter from a few staff members here at the eye clinic, a young man and two women. For a moment, it was a flashback to normalcy, to the easy camaraderie that has been suspended for now and will return when it's safe again.

March 31, 2020 – a possible alternative… why not a "stay-at-home" travel sketchbook!

April is Fake Journal Month (started by Roz Stendahl several years ago), and since this pandemic will postpone the idea I had of leading a Road Scholar "Travelers-with-Sketchbooks Tour," I've decided to create a whole sketchbook based on one of their website's itineraries, but without taking the actual trip! When this fake-journal sketchbook is done, I'll publish it on my blog and maybe offer it to Road Scholar for their marketing, to support them during this crazy time. I'm going to post-date it 2022, two years from now. Who knows if there will even be a world by then?

April 15, 2020

My fake journal is finished.

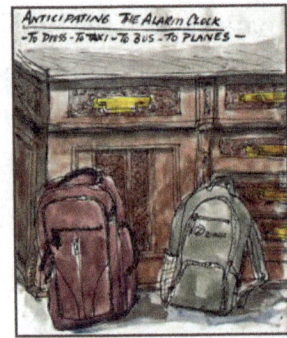 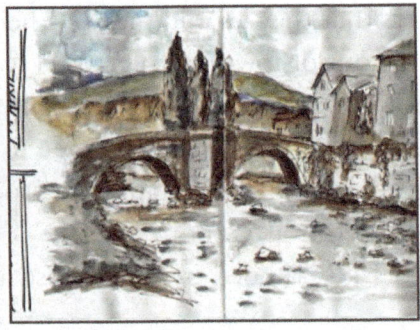

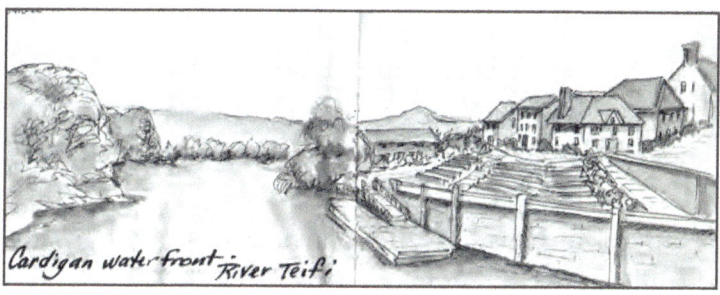

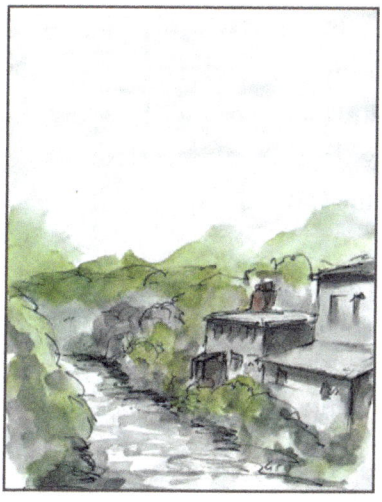

The story's narrative is handwritten in the sketchbook, all the info based on the Road Scholar itinerary, then fluffed out with further internet research. The notes and sketches feel authentic, as if I'd really been there. I even invented a few quirky characters to travel with me! I'll turn this into blog posts next, then send links over to Kelsey at Road Scholar.

It's so easy to stay quarantine-safe when you're retired with food in the fridge, ample art supplies, and an uncontrollable imagination.

April 22, 2020 - Tuesday

I've heard back from Road Scholar, saying they'd like to write a brief story about my "fake-journal way of traveling" on their blog! How exciting! The article is scheduled to be online around May first. Anything any of us can do to help businesses that are suffering right now is a good idea. Also, if making this silly fake journal and getting it out into the world helps even a single person find an oasis of peace in this crazy pandemic, I'm happy.

After quarantine, I wonder how my life will change, or even if it will? This introverted hermit artist/writer lifestyle suits me most days.

May 15, 2020 - morning pages

I learned recently that an old acquaintance is now marketing her services in editing, publishing, and book promotion. The next day, I learned that my cousin, a talented Florida artist, also has had a book published featuring her work. Then the following day, I heard two of my close creative circle friends talking about their next publishing projects. Three sparks in a row? Interesting.

It seems I'm living in the middle of a fertile field of creators, where I've longed to be forever, a place where I can grow. I know I'm an artist, and a blogger, but maybe there are other seeds to plant as well. I still have this dream of becoming a published author, but the memoir I've started about my childhood leaves me cold. The blog, *Aloft with Inspiration,* satisfies most of my writing urges for now, at least until I have something larger to put out into the world.

Quality memoirs aren't really about the author. Instead, they tell a tale about something perhaps universal, something that's important to share with the world. Something that's worth cutting down a tree to print it. I've always thought of that as an excellent litmus test: Is this worth killing a perfectly good tree?

Finding awe in the commonplace. If I ever write a memoir, that's what I'd like to write about.

May 16, 2020 - thoughts about "Consuming vs. Producing"

I can't read books, answer emails, catch up on the news, if I'm also trying to write and paint every day. Too much consuming makes me crave time producing. And of course, I'd better not overlook that essential fallow time in between the two.

I've learned there are now many ways to publish a book. Apparently, self-publishing is no longer synonymous with "vanity press." Instead, it's a respectable alternative to sending out endless pitch letters to agents, papering your bathroom walls with rejection letters, then finally getting a book deal with a small press who offers minor royalties and forces you to give up much of the control. These are things to ponder while I get on with daily life.

June 18, 2020 - Thursday

Another early summer morning, but it's the middle of Covid Days. A single car drives by, despite it being mid-week commuter time. The hum of large air conditioners, birds chattering in the distance, and farther away, the buzz of light traffic on the highway. I'm so lucky to live here on the third floor in the middle of town. When so many people are feeling isolated, I get to feel included, but still safe. I can walk around my neighborhood and the few people I see are in cars with their windows rolled up and air conditioners on. It's the automotive version of wearing a mask while social distancing. I have so many choices, even at this time when most people feel like they have so few.

I get to choose what to make of my circumstances, literally. Do I want to make up a story that has me starring as a victim, or as a hero? If, on some days, I'm only rescuing myself from my worst self, that can be heroic enough.

June 26, 2020 - next creative idea

I'm in Week 2 of Summer School in my creative circle group. The focus now is very gentle brainstorming; no plans yet, just pondering the questions in this week's lesson.

"What am I leaning toward for my next creative impulses?"

"What is drawing me?"

"What do I want to be?*"* (The answer to this question is simple: I want to be contented.)

"What do I want to do?*"* is an entirely different question!

"What do you want to finish by a year from now?"

"By a year from now, I want to have created a little booklet, very simple, based on my Kimball Jenkins lesson plans. Maybe call it *The Look at That Sketcher's Manual*. Dead simple."

Wow, where did that come from?! Now that I put into writing what felt like a crazy idea, I'm already scribbling out the table of contents. I can't write fast enough…

July 2, 2020 - early morning quiet excitement about making a booklet

I feel like I'm being both drawn and nudged to do this tiny book project. What a difference in energy I felt when I shifted my focus from dredging up that childhood memoir project to creating an easy-to-follow sketching manual.

This booklet idea started when I realized I worked so hard fine-tuning those art class lesson plans, and if I'm never going to teach again, they're all going to die on my laptop. And the way my eyesight is going, I may not have that long to see my laptop screen either!

The reason I started teaching in the first place, only three years ago, was clear. There simply were no in-person classes, nor any instruction books, whose primary goal was to streamline the journey from nervous beginner to playful, easy sketcher. The online courses from Sketchbook Skool were as close as I could get to what I was looking for, but I wanted more. I wanted to create a *local* community. I wanted to offer an in-person class with minimal technique and maximum enticement. Joyful enticement, not excruciating efforts!

Now the challenge is to transfer my effusive,

gesture-filled presentation into a booklet, maybe even a little book. Pithy little sentences are coming to me out of nowhere, crazy things like:

"The subject matter doesn't matter! You're learning to see, that's all!"

"Look! Look again! Start tracing what you see into your sketchbook with big juicy lines!"

I ask myself, what do I want to say more than anything?

What is this book's North Star?

I want the reader to know in their bones,

"There's no left-brain, linear secret to getting good at sketching.

You're learning how to get good at sitting around doing nothing. You've done that before, right?

The hardest part is giving your brain permission to calm down. Then you look around.

Then you take a breath. Then you put the tip of your pen on the paper.

Then look, breathe again, and simply caress the world."

But will they believe me? Unlikely.

Later that day…

I've made the rock-solid decision to leave my personal eyesight situation completely *out of my "Look at That!"* book.

It's obvious to me; the more art instruction I write, the more important I know it is. The entire focus of *Look at That!* needs to be on the excitement of seeing, that's all.

It was so aggravating to teach at Kimball Jenkins in March 2019 when my eyesight challenges distracted everyone, not just me, from the momentum of the art class. Now my enthusiasm can fly; my difficulty seeing is irrelevant. It's so empowering to present myself as an artist, an art teacher, with no red flag of disability leading the way. That may come out in a future book, but certainly not now.

I know writing this book, then getting it all the way through editing and designing, and across the finish line to publishing, will be a process with a million forks in the road. I know I'll be tempted to throw the whole thing in the trash more than once, especially if I listen to that old internal voice saying, *"Who do you think you are?"* That voice is vintage self-doubt.

Knowing that, I've decided to not have any schedule at all, to just work on the next tiny bit, as far as my very near-sighted single eye can see (metaphors come in so handy!). I need a little pleasurable momentum before I make any formal plans. In the past. long-range planning often killed my joy. I need to trick myself into thinking this new project is, "No Big Deal." Then I might actually complete it when I'm not looking!

I'm so grateful for the understanding from Syd Banks I came across in 2008. It taught me that every single minute of the day, I have the innate ability to observe my own thoughts and ask whether they're serving me well at this very moment. "Don't believe everything you think" is the best advice I ever got.

I bet a couple dozen pages printed at Staples will be

more than enough for this booklet called *Look at That!* We'll see.

July 5, 2020 - Sunday afternoon

My sketching time each Sunday afternoon with Patrick is so refreshing after a relentless week of rewriting lesson plans so they work as a booklet. Sketching on site with Patrick reminds me how rich an experience it is to sketch with others, rather than always on my own.

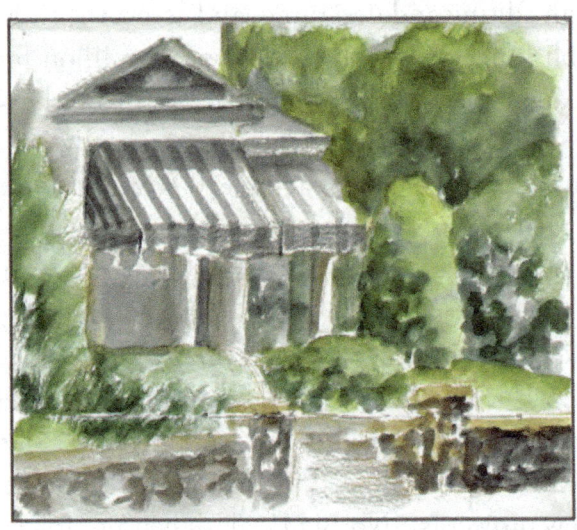

The other benefit of plein-air work is that you meet the nicest people when sketching in a neighborhood! Dave, the owner of this house, just came outside, introduced himself, and told us a bit of history about his home. Patrick, my architect buddy, asks the best questions, and I loved listening to them both.

July 31, 2020

The more time I put into this book project, the more I want it to be done right. I'm looking into places like BookBaby who help people self-publish while sparing writers the work of learning everything your book must navigate through to get from manuscript to landing right there in bookstores and on Amazon. I'm amazed at how much my initial vision for this book has expanded. It's all slowly coming together.

August 15, 2020 - Saturday late afternoon- two weeks later

I've been working like a madwoman, and just printed out my draft of the whole *Look at That Manual*. It's over 70 pages, with illustrations, and it was a struggle to keep it down to even that. Was I crazy to think all I had to say would fit into a couple dozen pages?

My in-person lesson outlines took up only four pages, but the dog-and-pony show that brings it all to life needs a lot more explanation. It's so hard to put it into words rather than simply showing: "Hold your brush like *this*, not *this*." That takes about three seconds to say, and half a page to describe in writing.

What next? Not totally clear. Production decisions will be interesting, and I have many more final book illustrations to complete.

August 23, 2020 - another Sunday outing

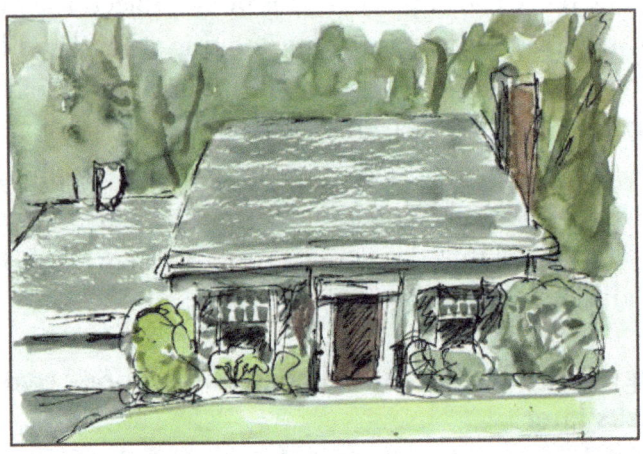

It's amazing how fast you can draw when a raindrop unexpectedly lands on your arm! I love starting with the fudé calligraphy pen and the tint brush, aiming for the largest overall shapes first. My Look-At-That Art Pouch came in handy for quick pen / brush changes. I designed the image area using GPS dots, (from the Chapter 3 lesson I just wrote in *"Look at That!"*) then roughed in the darkest darks. The basic structures satisfied me within five minutes, and I continued drawing until I felt those first few raindrops. I added color while sitting in the car during the downpour that followed our mad dash for cover.

Sketching is getting easier and easier, finally. Just like the joke about Carnegie Hall--- all it takes to get good at this is hundreds and hundreds of hours of enjoyable practice.

August 24, 2020

Every possible insecurity about *Look at That!* came out this week; my mind can be a real war zone. Nightmares, irritability, this feels like internal sabotage, because absolutely nothing is wrong! Luckily, mindsets never stay the same for long.

Continue waltzing forward, chin up, even when mildly lost.

August 25, 2020 - after the SPS webinar

I just finished a one-hour free webinar (which, of course, was a one-hour advertisement!) and I'm about to make a huge decision. The people who run and teach in *Self-Publishing School* are young, smart, and over-the-top enthusiastic. In my one-on-one phone call, I told the young man that he'd done a great job pitching the sale and I was excited, yet still had to "sleep on it" before I made the formal commitment. The course costs less than a full semester of college tuition, but also far more than I usually spend on any single item other than a car. It's expensive, and teaches so much material, far beyond what you need to know to simply *write* a book. That's the easy part really. This is an intensive *publishing* course, covering every single step along the way.

It feels right; it's a thorough, well-designed course of study. I just have to stop scaring myself. I know I can do this.

August 26, 2020 - the next day, 8:30am

It's official: I'm in. Gulp! I'm overwhelmed by what I need to learn, and my stupid brain is acting like there's a final exam in three days. How the heck did I ever make it through kindergarten?

September 1, 2020 - a week later

I'm binge-watching lessons, trying to fit it all into my skull. I just sent my first "request for quote" to a professional editor. I've changed and simplified the subtitle, and I like it much better now: *Discover the Joy of Seeing by Sketching.* Yes! That puts the horse squarely in front of the cart. The Joy of Seeing is the whole point... ahhh.

September 16, 2020 - late evening, exhausted

Marathon editing/rewriting day. It's amazing how everything is hooked together, and even the slightest change can inspire me to change or tweak even more in this book. It feels like all the times I've been sketching, and I needed someone to pull the brush out of my hand! Stop! Enough!

I just registered and paid for the book's ISBN and copyright number. Now it's official.

September 28, 2020 - perfect autumn day

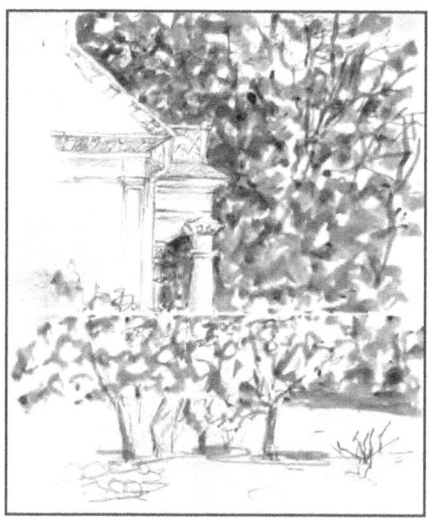

So good to be out sketching with Patrick after a few Sundays off. Starting with pencil was fun, I haven't done that in a long time. Then I continued with the tint brush and realized that was all the art tools I want to use today. Sometimes the less pre-planning I do, the better the sketch turns out. At times like this, it feels like I'm taking dictation via a spiritual Bluetooth device. "Trust your best instincts; let's keep it simple today." Makes me smile.

September 30, 2020 - big day

This morning I sent the final manuscript of *Look at That!* to the graphic designer. Another mile marker passed in this marathon. Now on to choosing the keywords and categories required for Amazon's search algorithms. Who, me? Yes Bobbie, you. I've learned so much in only a few weeks.

October 11, 2020 - Sunday

Today's sketch time took us to East Concord. Patrick was drawn to this entire building, and I especially liked the weathervane, even though I couldn't see it clearly.

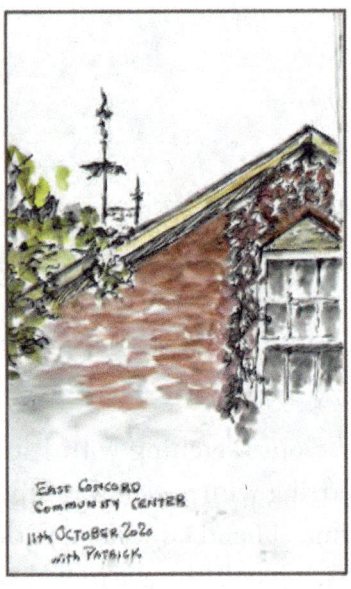

That's where loose sketching comes in: let the viewer do some of the work! Today was a cool, dry autumn day, and once again, this time-out for plein-air sketching is the perfect break from being chained to my computer, working on the graphic design details of the book. There are so many back-and-forth emails with the designer! I'm glad I hired a professional, of course, but I know he feels reined in by my insistence that the layout be a certain way.

Designing a book makes sketching a far-away lightning rod seem easy in comparison!

October 16, 2020 - Friday, 4:10 pm

I'm impressed they built so much book marketing into this self-publishing course. Naturally, they want their graduates to be successful; planning the book launch and follow-up is all part of it. The secret is to think of yourself as a business owner as well as an author. People who want to just be authors let someone else do all this work, but they give up much of the decision-making power as well. I have occasional grumbles, but no regrets.

October 25, 2020 - Sunday 3pm

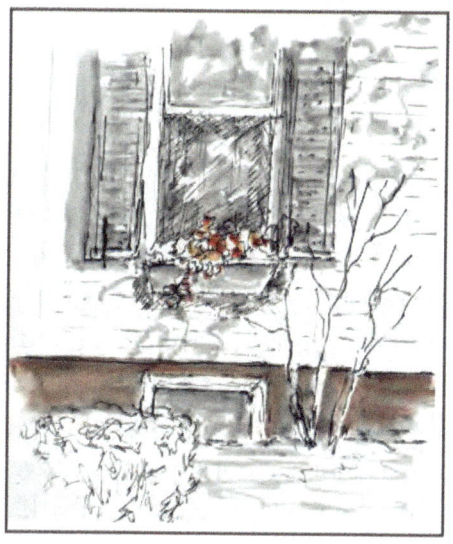

Still warm enough to sit outside and enjoy the beauty of the day. The owner of this house, and her neighbor, just stopped by to say a friendly hello and to see what we were doing. Leaf blowers and lawnmowers are the background music of the day.

I notice the shadows are getting longer earlier in the day, as the light shifts from summer to winter. The man across the street is spouting accusations at his un-cooperative yardwork equipment. The next instrument added to the day's orchestra is a vacuum cleaner in a driveway, a car being cleaned out. I smile. It all reminds me of Prokofiev's "Peter and the Wolf." Another beautiful day is done.

November 8, 2020

"T-Minus Two Weeks and counting" until the official launch day of November 22nd, 2020. There are so many gnarly details that go into self-publishing. I suppose if it were easy and inexpensive, everyone would do it.

I hired out some editing and the up-loadable file creation, and I'm so pleased with the brilliant cover design. The dozens of other steps to getting it out into the world have been up to me, and me alone. The early versions of the designer's layout might have been good enough for someone else, but they weren't right for me until the very end. I finally have a book I'm proud of.

I've learned as much about myself as I have about publishing. It'll be a long while before I embark on a second book, but as Self-Publishing School said, "This course is way too difficult and expensive if you only plan to write one book. If you're a career author though, this is the best way to go."

I suspect they're right.

November 12, 2020 - late afternoon

The first box just arrived. I can hardly breathe. Looks like all this work has been worth it.

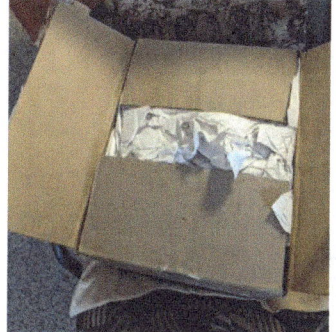
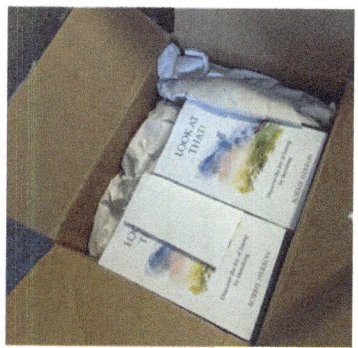
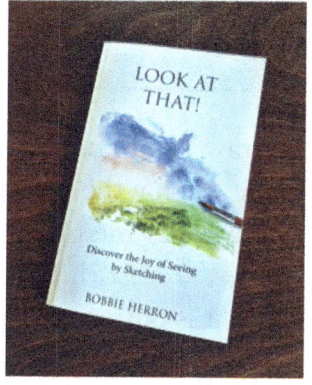

Most copies of this book, of course, will not have to pass through my home; they will be shipped directly from Amazon or sold through bookstores. The precious cargo in this single box is just for the outdoor book launch party in two weeks. That gathering's protocol will be clear: masking required, with mandatory social distancing, of course.

It's been stressful birthing this, baby. Time for tea.

November 16, 2020 - Monday

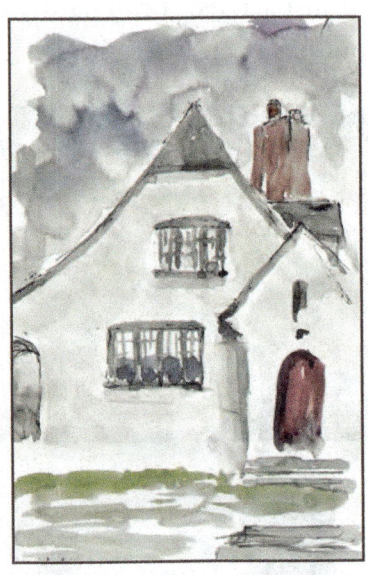

About 2pm, it's raw, cold, and cloudy, but Patrick and I are still out here, seizing the day by sketching. The swooping roofline reminds me of the seven dwarves' cottage in *Snow White,* at least the way I drew it! I can easily forget how cold it is outside when I'm having this much fun.

December 10, 2020 - 9:30pm

It's been a little over two weeks since I hit "publish" on this funny little book, *Look at That!* My friends from every walk of life, every possible connection to me, have been so kind, so generous with their enthusiastic response. I've sold many books online already, to total strangers, and blush at their poetic five-star reviews.

I know several of my readers flinch at claiming the

title of "artist;" it's utterly foreign to them. And yet many have also said, "After reading your book, I think I'll give it a try." I get choked up often.

December 11, 2020 - sketchbook notes

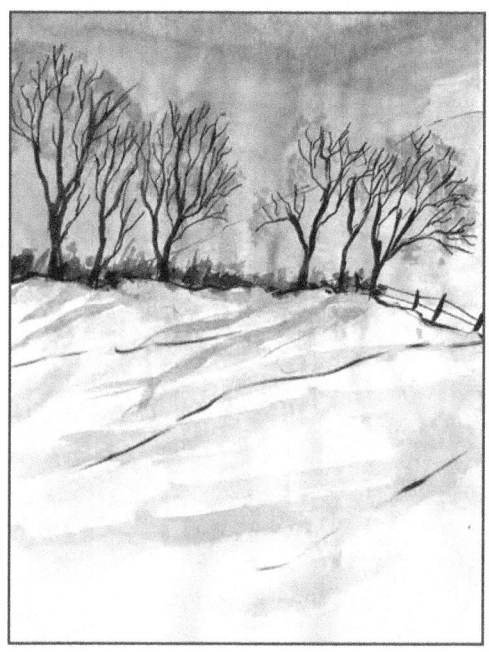

I just finished another assignment from one of my online classes. A rogue piece of Indian yellow watercolor paint must have been stuck between the hairs of my brush. I smile; my grey brushwork exercise has just been given an unexpected golden glow.

And really, isn't "the unexpected" one of the most predictable things in life?

I'm only starting to see that now, in these last few years. Big John used to say, *"Everything from the ears up is for entertainment value only."*

Perhaps everything between the hairs of the brush serves that same purpose: Unexpected Entertainment.

For me, the secret to a happy life is simple:

Keep Calm.

Carry On.

Carrying A Sketchbook Helps.

Epilogue

July 19, 2022 - 5:49pm - final edits on *Double Take*, this second book, are complete!

Writing this second book was intense. Writing a memoir, even an artist's memoir with a limited scope, has felt vulnerable, and of course, exhausting. I've lost track of how many weeks I spent rereading journals and sketchbooks, deciding what to include, transcribing, editing, rewriting, as well as scanning over 160 illustrations, color-correcting them, resizing them.

Through it all, one wonderful group of people have been on my mind, have been my North Star. That group is my readers, the people who purchased a copy of my first book, *Look at That!* Thanks to you, that book has been an Amazon #1 Best Seller for well over a year.

Your generous online reviews and private emails to

me through my website have touched my heart, and often brought me to tears. You restore my faith in humanity, especially during these recent tough months on our beautiful planet.

So thank you from the bottom of my heart. As the marketing material will state, *"This book is not everyone's cup of tea."* If you liked my first book, and are putting some of those lessons into practice, I hope this second book will take you one step farther down the road to becoming a contented, chronic sketchbook artist.

I'd like to leave you with a bit of advice, wrapped in a metaphor:

"Wash your glasses often."

Be present for what's happening in this very moment, and make room for the next adventure as well. Wash your glasses and open your heart. Do it again. Then again. And maybe... now too. A small art kit is good. Traveling light is wonderful. Minimal "baggage" in your mind and heart is best of all. Seeing your mental baggage is as simple as noticing that your glasses are dirty. Once you've noticed, it's obvious, thanks to doing a double take.

I'd love to hear from you. You can write to me via the contact link on my blog at www.aloftwithinspiration.com.

Your honest reviews of this book on Amazon help so much to get this book out into the world. I appreciate it.

A good double take can resurrect hope.

What's better than that?

Made in the USA
Las Vegas, NV
01 October 2023